Springburn to Lawers

Addressing the Journey

Springburn to Lawers

Addressing the Journey

MIKE DONNELLY

Story Terrace

For Mum and Dad

Always a Part of Us

CONTENTS

1. CAMPSIE STREET, SPRINGBURN: 1957 - 1965   11

2. BRODIE ROAD, BALORNOCK - PART 1: 1965 - 1972   21

3. BRODIE ROAD, BALORNOCK - PART 2: 1972 - 1979   31

4. CROWN STREET ABERDEEN – 1979   45

5. LIVING WITH STEVE: 1979 - 1980   51

6. ROSEMOUNT PLACE: 1980 - 1982   57

7. AUCHMILL ROAD - PART 1: 1982 - 1984   63

8. AUCHMILL ROAD - PART 2: 1984 - 1988   69

9. AUCHMILL ROAD - PART 3: 1988 - 1990   81

10. BINNIEHILL ROAD / CALDERWOOD GARDENS - PART 1: 1990   91

11. BINNIEHILL ROAD / CALDERWOOD   99
    GARDENS - PART 2: 1991

12. RHINDMUIR GROVE - PART 1: 1991 -   107
    1993

13. RHINDMUIR GROVE - PART 2: 1993 -   111
    1995

14. RHINDMUIR GROVE - PART 3: 1995 -   123
    1996

15. RHINDMUIR GROVE - PART 4: 1996 -   131
    1997

16. RHINDMUIR GROVE - PART 5: 1997 -   139
    2001

17. RHINDMUIR GROVE - PART 6: 2001 -   149
    2004

18. RHINDMUIR GROVE - PART 7: 2004   157

19. RHINDMUIR GROVE - PART 8: 2004 -   165
    2007

20. RHINDMUIR GROVE - PART 9: 2007 -   173
    2009

21. BOTHWELL ROAD - PART 1: 2009 –   179

2010

22. BOTHWELL ROAD - PART 2: 2010 - 2013   187

23. BOTHWELL ROAD - PART 3: 2013-2015   193

24. BOTHWELL ROAD - PART 4: 2015-2018   201

25. BOTHWELL ROAD - PART 5: 2018 – PRESENT   205

26. CROFTMORAIG - 2019   211

27. OLD LAWERS VILLAGE - 2021   215

28. REFLECTIONS ON MY LIFE   221

ACKNOWLEDGEMENT   229

1. CAMPSIE STREET, SPRINGBURN: 1957 - 1965

The city I was born into in 1957 was a city of smoke and dirt and poverty. There were tenement slums and tuberculosis and gaping holes left by the Second World War. Our games were played around the middens in the courtyard, and when we were cold, there was often no money for coal.

Some people born into my situation would have turned out badly. But Glasgow was changing on the back of the post-war boom, and I was born at the right time to take advantage of everything it was about to offer.

I came into the world on 29th December, 1957, just in time for New Year. I was the third son of Elizabeth and Frank Donnelly, who lived in a one-bed flat in Campsie Street in Springburn. It was cramped with the five of us, but it didn't stay that way for long. By the time my sister Marie was born there were eight of us squashed in together, with a single lavatory and barely enough beds to go round.

The 4 boys slept top 'n' tail in the bed together in the front room, and the girls slept in the bed recess in the same room. There was hardly any privacy and certainly no secrets! Mum and Dad had to make do with a makeshift bed in the small recess in the living area.

And it was cold. In the winter, we huddled together with coats on top of our blankets to keep us from freezing. And just the thought of getting up in the morning before the fire was properly lit was enough to make you cold to your bones. We had a single-bar electric heater, but that was only for emergencies when there was no money for coal or briquettes. I was careless once and left it on. I got clattered for that!

With so many kids, there was always something going on! Who knows how baby Marie ended up under the glass lightshade when it fell? All I remember was the chaos. Francis and Arthur ran to get my mum while I kept the little ones, Christine and Jim, away from the glass on the floor. There was blood everywhere, and Marie was screaming like mad! Mum was beside herself. Some of the neighbours must have run in to help, and Marie was rushed out of the house and taken to hospital. They were away for ages. We didn't know what to do with ourselves while we waited. Was she badly injured, and would we ever see her again? It was late when they finally brought her home. She was lucky. All she had to show for her adventure was a neat row of stitches. She still bears the scars behind her ear to this day.

My mum was a clippie on the buses before she met and married my dad. She was a strong woman – she had to be, with six children to raise and only one wage coming in. My dad was a scaffolder, and he often worked away at the hydro plants, going where the work was. So, we all had to pitch in where we could.

In my mind's eye, I can still see my mother carrying all our dirty clothes down two flights of stairs to the wash house and shouting out at us to 'mind the weans'. She used to insist on cleanliness, too. There was no bathroom in the flat, but there was a wooden bath that we used to drag out and fill with hot water in front of the fire. It was a real chore to heat the water in the scullery and carry it through to the bath over and over again until it was full.

And when the washing was done and the children were clean, she would sit down and mend what could be mended and handed down to the next in line. We were well warned to look after our clothes because they had to last. But when the last possible use was wrung out of them, they could go to the rag man. When I was very little, I was wary of the rag man with his big horse and cart, coming round the streets and shouting in his big voice. But as soon as I learned we could get pennies for old rags . . . We felt immensely rich when we swapped our tatty bundles for pennies!

Sometimes, we would take our money and run to the shop across the street to pick penny sweets from a tray or even − if we were particularly rich that day − something from the jars of sweets behind the counter. Sometimes, we would keep the pennies for a rainy day. And if we were lucky enough to be out when the gas man came round to light the streetlights, we would get a sweet from him for free.

One very special time, I was out walking with my mum and my aunt. A wee woman came up to us and gave me a 'christening piece'. This was an old tradition − when someone was on their way to a christening, they gave a 'christening piece' to the first person they met. It was for luck, and it was certainly lucky for me! I opened it quickly, excited to see what was inside. It was two wafer biscuits spread with butter and a half crown, all wrapped up together.

As kids, we had the run of the place, and once we were out, it was hard to get us back in! A tenement block with a shared courtyard was a place full of adventure. And if we got hungry, well, we would just shout up to the flat, 'Ma! Gie's a piece on jam!'

Mum would lean out of the window and drop it down to us, wrapped in paper. The trick was to catch it before it fell on the mucky ground!

We all shared what we had. The doors to the flats on the landing were always open, and we were in and out of each other's houses all the time.

There are some big events from that time that stick out in my memory. I remember Mum taking me and Arthur to Stobhill Hospital to get our tonsils out. It was very common in those days, and it was supposed to prevent ear and throat infections, which could be serious. I was four, and Arthur was five. We had to walk to the hospital, and I was worried and a bit scared all the way there. We had no idea what they were going to do to us in the hospital. There were rows of beds with children we didn't know, and some of them were crying. Mum wasn't allowed to stay with us, and that made it worse. I don't know how I would have got through it if it hadn't been for the nurse who looked after us. She was so beautiful and so nice to me that I fell in love with her straight away. My throat was sore after the operation, but she fed me ice cream and soothed away the pain. She made such an impression that I never forgot her or how she made me feel.

My first day at school was another big event. I think I was excited and scared at the same time. I thought it would be OK because my brothers were there, but I was scared to be on my own in a big classroom with a strange teacher. Mum took me to school, and I remember I didn't want her to go and leave me behind. I cried when she gave me a last hug and sent me inside. I just wanted to go home.

The school was called St Martha's, and my teacher was Mrs McCrossan. She was the headteacher, so she had to be strict, but she was nice at the same time. Once I settled down, it wasn't so bad. I thought it was funny there were two other boys called Michael in my class – Michael Began and Michael Meegan – and before long, the three Michaels became inseparable.

We got up to all sorts of tricks. In those days, policemen patrolled the streets and they knew everybody on their beat. There was a police box on the corner where the 'polisman' used to sit to write up his notes, and there was a phone for people to call the police station if they needed help. We used to dare each other to open the flap and speak into the phone. Then we would run away, giggling fit to burst. It was a risky thing to do. What if whoever answered it recognised our voices? What if they told the local cop and we got caught? Would we go to jail? How daring were we!

Springburn Park wasn't too far away, and there was so much to do there, especially in the summer! It was really huge. There was a bandstand and a cricket oval and three big ponds. One of them had boats. It had a hothouse that was called the Winter Gardens and it was always warm in there. It was full of strange plants that came from far-away countries.

It was paradise for a bunch of kids.

In the long summer holidays, we used to go fishing for sticklebacks in the ponds. That needed a lot of preparation. You had to get a jar for the fish and another jar for the worms, then you had to dig the worms up and put them in the jar. That worked best if the ground was wet, or it had been raining. Then you had to find a stick — it had to be the right size — and tie a bit of string on the end. Add a hook and one of the worms, and you were ready to go. The sticklebacks were easy to catch, but there was still the thrill of excitement as you watched one come up to the worm and take a nibble. You had to hold the stick really still in case you frightened it away. And then — yes! It took the hook, and you had to pull it in really quickly and grab it before it slipped off. I got very good at taking the hooks out of their little mouths. Any sticklebacks we caught, we put in jars. Once, I caught a perch. I wanted to keep it, but there were no spare bowls big enough. The only place I could think of to put it was the cistern above the toilet. I was pleased with my idea, but I hadn't thought it through. I had forgotten how many times the toilet would be flushed with eight people in the flat, and the perch didn't last long in there before it died. I suppose it didn't really have much of a chance.

Even though we had lots to do, there were times when we got bored. And when that happened, the pigeons in our neighbourhood had better watch out. On the half-landing of the tenement, there was a window. We would make a noose out of a bit of string, and we would lay it on the open windowsill and put down some crumbs of bread for bait. Then we would wait, hardly daring to move. A pigeon would land on the sill. It would look at us with beady eyes, then eye the breadcrumbs. It must have looked like an easy meal. And they were used to people being around. The minute the pigeon stepped on the noose, we would tighten it, and the pigeon would be caught! What happened to them after that depended on our mood. Sometimes we took them to a local pigeon fancier who had a big 'dookit'. Sometimes we killed them.

Sometimes, if we could scrape together enough money, we would go to the Prince's Cinema in Springburn. This was a great treat. I remember going to see *The Greatest Story Ever Told* with Arthur. We paid to get in with jam jars! Those were the days!

I quite liked primary school. As I got older, I had a new teacher, Mrs O'Hare. I fell in love with her because she reminded me of the nurse who had been so kind to me.

My memories of that time are mostly happy. My family were close, and I was never short of things to do or people to play with. Life was good. But things were about to change, and in a very short time, my young life would be touched by tragedy.

*L/R: Francis, Mum, Marie, Me, Arthur, Jim, & Christine in Campsie Street
circa 1964.*

Christmas in Campsie Street circa 1964. L/R: Francis, Marie, Me,
Arthur, Christine and Jim.

Mum and Dad on their wedding day with the cake. They married on 8th August 1953.

2. BRODIE ROAD, BALORNOCK - PART 1: 1965 - 1972

The cramped conditions in the tenement flat were finally too much for our large family. In 1965, we left Springburn behind and moved to Balornock. We moved into the bottom flat in a block of four, so we had a front and back garden to ourselves. But what was more, it had three bedrooms and a bathroom – what luxury!

It was a cause for celebration, so my mum and dad threw a housewarming party. It was a real shindig. Everyone we knew turned up. All the family came along. It was catered by the Co-op, so all my mum had to do was enjoy herself. Who knew where the money came from, but also – who cared? We might have worn hand-me-down clothes and had holes in our shoes, but we knew how to throw a party!

It was fun at first, but we kids soon got bored with the adult talk. There was a garden and new places to explore, and we had our cousins to help us! I don't remember the game, but I know that I was running away, taunting them to catch me. I ran towards the house, planning to get inside and hide, maybe. But my brother was too quick. He darted in front and got to the door first. He slammed the door closed and locked it just as I got there. There was no chance that I would stop. I pushed out my hand and it went straight through the glass, tearing into my wrist. I didn't realise it but what a commotion it caused.

All the adults came running. There was blood on my face and all over my clothes. I can still remember how the colour drained from my mother's face. Someone grabbed me and bundled me into a car. Someone else held cloths to my cuts to stem the bleeding. I remember how fast the car went as they rushed me to Stobhill Hospital and how bright the lights were in the accident and emergency department. I needed 13 stitches in my wrist. I've still got the scars.

As if that wasn't enough to cope with, the move itself was traumatic. Everything was different, and we knew nobody. And that wasn't all. We had a new little brother, Brian, who was born in Stobhill hospital. Luckily it was only a mile and a half from the old flat, so we could walk back to see our old friends when it all got too much. It took a few months before we started to meet people in the area, and going to a new school helped with that.

Eventually, we made new friends, and for my brother Jim and me, they were Tommy Smyth and Robert Morrison. Living in a new place gave us new lands to explore, and we used to go off on adventures for hours at a time, sometimes even for whole days. We were never missed. In those days, the adults didn't care where you went, as long as you were home before it got dark.

Left to our own devices, we were always getting into trouble. Usually, we managed to sort it out – or at least run away! But one day, our bravado had fatal consequences.

It was just a normal late summer's day. We had nothing much to do, so we decided to go exploring. We walked for miles, just messing about and climbing trees. Tommy threw a branch and marked where it landed. Then he said words I have never forgotten. 'If I fall and die today, put this on my grave!'

On the way home, Tommy and Jim decided to climb an electricity pylon. There were signs warning of the dangers, of course, but they ignored them. We were young – what could possibly happen to us? Tommy was quicker than Jim, and he raced ahead. They were just climbing, getting higher and higher, laughing and shouting out to each other.

Suddenly, there was a big flash. Smoke and sparks filled the air. Jim appeared through the smoke – he had managed to jump clear. He had landed hard, but he was OK.

Tommy was electrocuted and died instantly. He must have touched the wires as they climbed.

We didn't know what to do. Tommy was just hanging on the pylon. We had no way to get him down. We panicked. Not knowing what else to do, we ran home.

All the electricity in the street was out. People came out to find out why there was no electricity. They knew it was us. Everybody was out in the street, shouting, 'What have youse done?' But we rushed past them and went straight home to bed. We said nothing about Tommy, not even to each other.

The next day, the police came to the school. They called me out of class for questioning. It turned out somebody had known us, and of course, his mum knew he had been out with us. I had to explain what had happened and how we had been terrified and panicked and run away.

Tommy's mum never blamed us. At the funeral, she was really nice to us and gave us some money. The story was in the papers and everything. He was only nine years old.

It was my first experience of death, and it made a big impression on me. But it was not to be my last.

Henry O'Neil was another boy who lived around the corner. Buses used to be open at the back where people got on, and he used to jump on the back of the bus and hang on for a free ride. Then the buses all change to 'OMO' (one man operated) buses, which had doors at the front. Henry decided to give it a go. He jumped on the doors, but there was nowhere to hold on to, not really. He clung on until the bus turned left, and he lost his balance and fell off. The bus ran him over, and he died of his injuries.

The years passed, and friendships changed. When I was about 14, I was friends with Mark McLeod, who moved into the house along the road. I thought he was so cool because he did a needle and ink tattoo on his own arm. I was so impressed I got him to do one on my arm, too. He did it on his kitchen table.

We were always getting into trouble – more serious trouble now that we were older. We used to steal cars and go joyriding. There was nothing like the excitement of tearing through the streets at night, always listening in the back of your mind for sirens behind you. No doubt he was a bad influence on me for a while, but even I had my limits.

One day, I had nothing much to do, so I went round to his house for him. I thought we might go out, see what was going on. I walked into his room, and the smell of solvent hit me right away. He was lying in bed, like a zombie, with a bag of glue. I never had any time for that sort of thing, so I didn't need to think twice. I turned around and walked out. That was us done. Sadly, a couple of years later, he took it too far. He overdosed on glue and died.

By then, of course, I was at high school. I went to St Mungo's Academy, the same as my brothers. It was founded by the Marist Brothers in 1858, and the teachers were still priests. It was great because I got a bus pass for free. I got the bus to Castle Street all the way from home and back. How grown up was I, getting the bus to school!

St Mungo's was more regimented than primary school. Not many of my friends went there, and I couldn't understand why I had to. It was a boys-only school, and the teachers were very strict and hard on us. I didn't like it at all. And it didn't help that I got bullied. I had grown really quickly and was tall for my age. Besides that, I had red hair. I really stood out, and they made sure I paid for it.

I dodged school whenever I could. One of my tricks was to make up fake letters. It worked for a while, but I got careless and got caught. It was my own fault – I had handed in four letters that said, 'Granda has died.' Even I couldn't explain away that one!

Eventually, I was given an attendance card. This meant the teachers for each class had to sign to say I had turned up for their class. It felt like punishment because it was the last place

I wanted to be. It was suffocating, and I wanted out as soon as possible. The day I turned 15, there was no stopping me. I walked out with no qualifications and no idea what to do with my life, but I was free.

I needed to start making my own money and contributing to the family coffers. But I was tired of always just scraping by. I was old enough by then to know that I wanted a better life. And the only way to do that was to make as much money as I could. I decided I would do whatever it took to make my fortune.

It started with a paper round and delivering paraffin for people's heaters. That was OK for a while, but it wasn't enough. My next idea was to take stuff from the fields on the outskirts of the town and sell it round the doors. I knew people would take it off my hands if it was cheaper than in the shops. And they did. I would take anything that was in season – potatoes, turnips, apples, rhubarb . . . That brought in a bit more. Then there were the bikes. I used to rebuild old bikes and sell them on. I had to try them out myself, of course, just to make sure they were safe. I just ran them down the road and back. Once, I was trying one out, and the wheel came off. I nearly died!

I worked hard all week, and by the weekend, I would have maybe £5 in my pocket. I would send my brother to the ice cream van for me and give him 50 pence for going. That felt good.

I would do almost anything to earn a coin, but I never crossed too far over the line except for one time when temptation got too much. At chapel one Sunday, I noticed there was a thruppence stuck in the slot of the collection box. I thought about it for a while, and I decided it was meant to be. If the church had needed the money, it would have gone right in. So, I dug it out and pocketed it. On the way home, I bought an apple from the shop. I was happily eating it when all of a sudden I felt a sharp pain. It was a wasp, and it had stung me! That was the judgement – it was God's wasp! So, no more stealing for me!

Jim Marshall was the best fighter in the street. I was scared of him, even though I was bigger than him. One day, he challenged me to a fight. I was wearing my good barathea jacket and didn't have time to take it off. I fought with it on. And I won! But the jacket was ripped up the back. I didn't care. When I got home, I told my mum about the fight, proud that I had won. She wasn't impressed – she battered me because I had ripped my jacket! That brought me back down to earth! Jim and I became good pals after that.

Me outside our front door at Brodie Road. I would go on to cut my wrist on one of the glass panels on the door.

Me and my pal Jim Marshall thinking we were cool.

L/R: Me, Jim and Robert Morrison with our pal Tommy Smyth (inset) by the pylon where Tommy died aged 9 years. 1966.

3. BRODIE ROAD, BALORNOCK - PART 2: 1972 - 1979

The whole family was growing up and starting to find their way in the world. My brother Francis was studying to be a priest, though later he would give it up and become an languages teacher, working across the world. He used to get the whole family together in one room to pray, and he would collect any stray pennies for the orphans in Africa. Of course, as a priest, he would never make any money, and that didn't appeal to me! My brother Arthur was an electrician, and he got £5 a week. It was a steady job, not like me, running around with all my tricks, trying to scrape together enough for the weekend. I was jealous. I decided I wanted to be an electrician too.

Unfortunately for me, there were no opportunities with the electricity board. But I wanted a proper job. I was tired of trying to make a penny every which way. So, I went along to the careers advice people, and they said I could be apprenticed to the gas board and train to become a gas engineer if I passed the aptitude test. I had never heard of a gas engineer, but I went along with it. I thought, *What have I got to lose?*

If only I had known how this decision would shape my life!

The aptitude test was held in George Square. I gave it my best shot, and I was successful! Not only that, but I was the first apprentice to be accepted by the gas board without any O-grades.

Suddenly, I had a proper job and a date to start it. I would be earning £9 per week, which was better than Arthur! I was quite proud of myself. The only downside was they told me to get a haircut before I started work, so my 'afro' had to go. Dad got the clippers out and gave me a skinhead cut. It was freezing without my lion's mane of hair to keep me warm!

Being an apprentice was all about learning on the job, but I had to get my qualifications, too. I ended up in the College of Building and Printing in Parkhead. It was a block release from the gas board, so I was working and learning at the same time. I had lots of fun at college. I was a natural, and I picked it up very quickly. I had been used to putting bikes together and making things, so lead soldering joints came naturally, and my instructors were so impressed they showed my work around the college. It was embarrassing, but I was chuffed, too.

I enjoyed my apprenticeship, and I worked hard. I used to practise gas servicing on Mum's fire and back boiler – I used to strip it down and rebuild it at least twice a week. And I learned how to reverse the gas coin meter so it ran backwards. That meant there was no charge for gas. I thought I was doing a good thing, saving money. Mum didn't know – I don't think she would have approved!

One day, when she was out, I took the whole fireplace apart. Mum went mental when she came home. I had to figure out how to rebuild it pretty smartly. I had some cement, but I needed sand, so I acquired it from a bunker at the local golf course. Needs must!

I was learning all the time. At work, I was always asking questions. They thought this was a good thing, and so did I. It's the only way to learn. That is something I've carried through life, always. I always ask questions, and I tell people to do the same – because if you don't ask, you don't get!

But it wasn't all work and no play. We were young, we were earning and we wanted to have a good time. I was tall for my age, so the others would send me into the shop to get alcohol for them. At the weekends, we used to go to the dancing. Our favourite place was Tiffany's in Sauchiehall Street.

I was very particular about my clothes in those days. I always had to have the latest fashion, even though I had no taste whatsoever! It was the '70s, and I dressed to impress. I remember going out dressed in sky-blue trousers and a yellow jumper, with stack-heeled boots. They made me so tall I had to crouch to get on the bus. Mum would always tell me to stand up straight! But I thought I looked the business!

When I wanted something new, Mum would get me a Provident cheque for £40. This was like a loan that could be paid back over time. Then I would go into the city and buy clothes. I don't know if it was because I had been used to wearing hand-me-downs all my life, but now I had some money, I would only wear something once. Then I would throw or give it away and ask Mum to get me another cheque. Mum used to complain about that, but I didn't care too much. New clothes were a luxury I had earned.

Everything happened at Tiffany's! One night, I was standing on the balcony, and I felt a tap on my shoulder. I turned around. It was an Asian guy with big eyes and a big smile. He said his name was Joey, and he offered to buy us all a beer.

'OK!' Never say no to free beer! We started chatting. It turned out his name was really Balwinder Gill, and he was trying to make friends. His family were into restaurants, and Charan Gill, the founder of the famous Ashoka chain of Indian restaurants, was his brother.

Over time, we got really friendly with him. We even went on holiday together to a caravan park in Berwick-upon-Tweed. We got friendly with his family, too. They taught me to make *pakora*. It was interesting to see a different culture in our home city, especially at that time. The food was so different to what I was used to, and so was the music. Even now, when I hear *bhangra* music, I think about that time. He is still a family friend today.

Being around wealthy people opened my eyes. I noticed early on how money opened doors, and I wanted that for myself. It made me even more determined to get on and make something of my life. I decided I would be a millionaire before my 50th birthday, no matter what it took to get there.

We went to Tiffany's to dance and let our hair down, but mainly we went to meet girls. It was called 'getting a lumber', and I suppose I got my fair share. None of them were serious. And then one night I met a girl called Ann. We got to talking, and I remember at the end of the night, we left the club together and walked to George Square. She lived in

Baillieston, and her mum was German. She gave me her number, and I wrote it on a £5 note because it was all I had. We said goodnight and went our separate ways.

And then I spent the £5 note!

Somehow, though, we managed to get in touch. We saw each other a few times, but we didn't get together properly until my mum and dad's silver wedding anniversary in 1977. I invited Ann to come as my date for the night, and that was when we became a couple.

My dad liked a pint and to place a bet. When he went out on a Saturday afternoon, he took me and Arthur with him. I can still remember the atmosphere in the pub when there was a big race on. It would be into the bookies to place a bet, then into the pub for a pint and to see how the racing went. And then the same over again. It was no coincidence that bookies' shops were opened next to pubs! Although Arthur was older than me, he didn't get into the pub because he didn't look old enough. He could get into the bookies, though, and that was the beginning of a lifetime habit. Even these days, he still bets too much. I gave up betting before the end of my apprenticeship. I didn't see the point. Wasting money on fruitless bets was never going to get me on in life.

There was the occasional win, though, and that was enough to keep my dad and Arthur going back. Once, my dad won a substantial amount on one of the 'ITV 7' races. It was enough for him to lend me £130 to buy my first car. I didn't have a licence, but I was getting lessons and I knew how to drive.

I got the car for £125. It was a second-hand clapped-out Mini. I was very pleased with it, but not for long. I had to push it every morning to get it started. One night, it got broken into, and the transistor radio was stolen from inside. After that, I thought the car might get stolen, so I started taking the alternator out at night. One day, I forgot to put it back, and I pushed the car for ages before I remembered. That was the final straw. It had to go.

Eventually, a dealer offered me £30 for it, and I took it. I gave him the logbook, and he said he would change the ownership papers. A week later, I was asleep in bed when the whole family was wakened by banging on the door. It was 5 a.m. Who comes to the door at that time? It must be an emergency. Dad opened the door, and it was the police, looking for me! They dragged me out of bed and down to the police station. It was terrifying. I had no idea what was going on. It turned out that the car that I could hardly get to run had been used as a getaway car in a robbery – and it was still registered under my name! It took a lot of explaining before they were satisfied!

The four years of my apprenticeship soon passed, and I got my gas engineer's licence. I had enjoyed being an apprentice, but now it was time to move into the real world of work.

As the new boy, I was teamed up with a few different engineers, but eventually, I was teamed with George Campbell, who was a driving engineer. This meant he had a van to get around. Other engineers were walking engineers, so they had to take the bus to get to jobs. George was a nice chap, and he would let me practise driving in the van. That meant he could have a beer at lunchtime while I drove. In fact, it was often more than just one beer. The engineers in those days had figured out that they could do their jobs and still have plenty of time to spare for other pursuits – even other jobs. One of the engineers ran The Grapes pub in Paisley Road West while he was supposed to be working for the gas board. All the engineers and a lot of my pals went there for a lock-in in the afternoon. After the pub, I would drive George back to work and then home. When I had dropped him off, I could take the van home with me and pick him up again in the morning. That was good because it meant I had the van all night and at weekends. I still hadn't passed my test at this time, so if I had been caught, George and I would both have been in trouble.

One Friday night, my pals and I were going to the dancing, and we went to the Nairn Bar in Auchinairn first. There were six of us. I was driving the van. One guy sat in the passenger seat, and the rest piled in the back. There were no seats; they just had to make space among the tools. The guys had had a few beers and were in a good mood. They were singing and having a great time.

We were driving down Auchinairn Road, and they kept egging me on to go faster. Sure enough, I went faster, and I started messing around, swinging the wheel left and right. They were bouncing around, trying to keep hold of the sides of the van, and I was swinging the wheel more and more wildly to wind them up . . . Of course, I lost control. In a shocking instant, the van veered off the road and crashed into the golf course wall. There was a moment of silence that seemed to stretch out forever as we tried to take in what had happened. Then the shouting started.

The wall was wrecked, and so was the front of the van. Jim Marshall had been thrown out of the back, and he lay there on the road, bleeding. It was carnage. I didn't know what to do. I had no licence, and now my job was on the line because I shouldn't have been driving the van. A passerby called the emergency services. It didn't take them long to respond. I could hear sirens in the distance, getting closer all the time.

My pals told me, 'Get out of here!'

I didn't have time to think it through. I panicked and did what they said. I ran away. Just like I had with Tommy.

Jim had a fractured skull and ended up in intensive care. I was terrified he might not pull through because the accident was all my fault. And what about George? He had let me take the van. He was a great guy, and he was getting old. The last thing I wanted was for him to lose his job because of me.

I phoned him and told him to report the van stolen.

I spent the next few days in hiding. Then I saw sense. I realised I had to face up to the consequences of my actions. I went to the police station and admitted stealing the van. I was charged with 'unauthorised taking of a vehicle'. Naturally, I got sacked, but George kept his job. Some of the guys were unhappy about this because George let me take the rap. But what else could I do?

I was blacklisted by Scottish Gas. That meant that not only was I sacked, but I couldn't get a job with any of the contractors who worked for them.

I had to sign on the 'buroo' – unemployment benefit. But I had been selling the odd bit of stuff to a plumber I knew, and he gave me a job on the side, cash in hand. It was mainly plumbing and bathrooms, but it was money coming in.

It took a while to find work in my field. Everywhere I tried in Glasgow knew I was blacklisted. Finally, I had a lead at a company called Gaswise. I called their office, and they told me to call back. So, I did. But I called the wrong company. It turned out Gaswise had a very similar number to another company called Maclean & Nuttall, and they were the ones who took my call. It was a mistake that would impact the course of my life, because, as it happened, Maclean & Nuttall also had a vacancy for a contractor. They told me I could start with them in Aberdeen or Barrow-in-Furness. Well away from Glasgow. I picked Aberdeen because I had never heard of Barrow-in-Furness.

That was the Thursday or Friday. I was told to get myself to Aberdeen for the following Monday. The job was supposed to last six weeks, but it was better than nothing, and who knew what it might lead to? Little did I know that those six weeks would turn into years.

I didn't even have a suitcase. Why would I? We never went on holiday. Mum borrowed a holdall from Auntie Vera, and I packed my clothes and tools. I was finally leaving home and heading out into the world, hopefully, to make my fortune – or at least make a start! It was a good feeling, but I couldn't help the nerves that bubbled up every time I thought about it. And I was leaving them all behind – Mum, Dad, my girlfriend, Ann – but it would be worth it to finally have a job.

The family all came to the station and waved me off on the train. As they disappeared into the distance, I hoisted up the bag and the strap broke from the weight of my tools. I could only hope it wasn't an omen!

Me and my pal Joey on holiday in a caravan at Berwick on Tweed.

Mum and Dad celebrating their Silver Wedding Anniversary by cutting the cake in 1978.

Double Silver Wedding Anniversary in 1978. L/R: Uncle Frank, Auntie Vera, Mum & Dad.

4. CROWN STREET ABERDEEN – 1979

The train journey seemed very long, but I eventually got to Aberdeen. It was a very different city from Glasgow. I was a bit shell-shocked as I walked down the platform. I was new to town, and everybody was a stranger. I had left behind my family, my home and my girlfriend, and for the first time in my life, I had only myself to rely on.

I was met by a guy called John Sparks. He was the man in charge at Maclean & Nuttall, and he was a Geordie. He took me to my digs at Crown Street and left me to get on with it. 'One of the lads will bring you to work in the morning,' he barked as he turned on his heel.

It was a guest house, a bed and breakfast place. It was dingy, and I had to share the toilets with the other residents. No such thing as en-suite in those days! And I had to pay for it myself. But accommodation was hard to get in Aberdeen, and at least I had somewhere to lay my head. I tried hard not to feel homesick.

Left on my own, I went for a wander. I found the Brentwood pub right next door, so I had some fish and chips and went for a beer. I wondered what would become of me in this strange new town, but I wasn't left alone to wonder for too long. In the pub, I met Paul Mitcheson, who was also a Geordie, and he worked for Maclean & Nuttall, too. He was a bit of a character. He had split up from his wife, and she told their kids he was dead. It was a friendship made to last – we still write to each other to this day.

I went to bed feeling a bit better. At least there would be one friendly face the next day.

In the morning, I was picked up and taken to Cotton Street, where the gas board was. It was down by the docks and the esplanade, and the area was quite run down. I couldn't help but be apprehensive.

I took a deep breath and went in.

There were maybe 20 other guys milling around, and it took me a few minutes to find John Sparks among them. They were all contractors from England, and I had never heard so many different accents in one place! Later, I found out that Scottish Gas couldn't supply enough engineers to cover all the work they had, so they subcontracted to Maclean & Nuttall and Gaswise. Maclean & Nuttall were based in Liverpool, and they sent contractors to Aberdeen from all around the country.

The gas board also employed a lot of locals. They treated the contractors like me as second-class citizens and kept us segregated from the other employees. We were paid more, but we had worse conditions and we got all the dirty jobs.

Although I had finished my apprenticeship just before I got sacked, I had no real experience. Regardless, I was given the keys to an old red van and handed a map of work and told to get on with it. Right in at the deep end. It was very surreal.

In my old job in Glasgow, I was given some work, and when it was done, I got sent home while the other guys played football or went to the pub, and then I came back again at 4 p.m. to clock out. Life was so different as an independent gas engineer. I had to work a lot harder for a start! I knew nothing about the place, the people or the appliances I was to work on. Besides that, I was living on my own for the first time. Homesickness was hard to fight off, and I was glad when Friday came around and I could drive home to Glasgow. It took four hours each way, but it was worth it to see my family and Ann and to have some home comforts, even for just a couple of days. That was the first of many hundreds of Friday night journeys to Glasgow. For a while, it was all I had to look forward to, until I started to make some friends in Aberdeen.

It was traumatic to begin with, but I just had to get on with it. And I quickly got into the way of things. The engineers and the technicians were OK, and I soon got to know them well enough.

We worked hard, and we played hard. We used to be regulars at the Champers Nightclub in Peterculter just outside Aberdeen, and it always ended up in a fight. Sometimes they could be brutal. Once John Sparks got into a fight and got stabbed in the heart. It came within an inch of killing him but somehow, he survived. He was off work for a long time. Three weeks after he came back to work, we went to the pub, and he insisted on driving home even though he was drunk. He lost control of the car and went into a tree. He was killed instantly. His death was meant to be. He was only 33 when he died.

All of his family came up to Aberdeen, and we got time off for the funeral. A collection tin was set up in the office for his family. Someone broke in through the window and stole it. It turned out it was one of the engineers. I was horrified because it was the collection for our dead colleague's family that was stolen. How could anyone do such a thing? Of course, he was sacked.

Once I settled in, I found the job interesting, and I liked the money, though again, I felt it wasn't enough. I had to pay for my own fuel, and the cost for digs seemed a lot for what it was. Breakfast was bacon and eggs, and there were always little flecks in the eggs. I found out why when I saw the cat sitting on the grill to keep warm, leaving hairs behind in the food.

I had to get out.

Me with my first Maclean & Nuttall van outside Ann's Mum & Dad's house circa 1979.

5. LIVING WITH STEVE: 1979 - 1980

Steve was a friend I made in Aberdeen, and we were both in digs. He felt the same as me about digs – it was far too expensive for what we got. There had to be another option. We got to talking, and somehow we got this idea to move out of our digs and stay in a caravan. We thought it would be better and cheaper, and it would give us some space and some freedom. No more landladies with strict rules and questionable food!

The place we picked was a caravan park near the village of Kirkton of Skene, at Westhill. It was bleak. Kirkton of Skene was just a farming village with only one pub. The caravan itself was in the middle of a field, and it had no bathroom. There was only a shower and toilet block that was shared with the whole site. That meant a trip outside no matter what the weather. It was always damp and cold, and there was no hot water. And never mind the spiders! They, at least, loved the place! The only heating in the caravan was a Calor gas heater, and the lights also ran off Calor gas, so that was another expense, but it still worked out cheaper than digs. Steve and I took turns cooking. It was always Campbell's meatballs from a can with spaghetti. Cheap and cheerful!

When I got settled, Ann came up for the weekend. She hated it from first sight, and that was not helped by the cold shower and the spiders! It was a miserable weekend, and she never came back to the caravan again. If I wanted to see her, I had to drive home.

The only saving grace was the pub in the village. We used to play pool against the locals for beer, and that helped the bar takings! It also helped take the edge off the fact that the caravan itself was miserable and damp. I was just as unhappy there as I had been in the digs. It was no better, even if it was cheaper.

Steve and I suffered it for a couple more months until I reversed a friend's van into someone else's car. That was it − the farmer told us to leave at once.

We were desperate. We had to find somewhere else at short notice, and that turned out to be Marywell Caravan Park, which was on the other side of Aberdeen, near Portlethen.

This caravan was worse than the last one! It was dire. It had a big sloping roof that leaked, so we struggled to keep our stuff dry. It did have a wee bathroom inside, though, which was a big improvement. Even though the bath was tiny and hard for a man of my height to get into, it was lovely to be able to have a hot bath. It was the only time I was warm that whole winter!

It was grim. After a couple of months, we decided to give up on the caravans and look for a flat together.

We ended up in a flat at Rosemount Place. It was four stories up, which was not a problem at first, though getting up all those stairs was a struggle coming home from the pub! It came furnished, and we each had our own bedroom. Luxury! It was such a big difference from the caravans! It was worth the extra cost.

It was in a good location, too. It was close to the city centre, and there were lots of pubs nearby. We were two young lads living alone, so there was lots of drinking and we had lots of parties! The flat was perfect for entertaining all our friends. By this time, I was earning £6 per hour, and I worked a 40-hour week, so I had plenty of spare cash to enjoy myself.

I still travelled to Glasgow almost every weekend. Sometimes, Ann came up to stay at the flat instead, and she got on well with my friends. I found I liked having her around.

Eventually, it got serious between us. In 1980, we were married at St Francis Chapel in Baillieston, with the reception in the church hall at St Bridget's. It was quite a big wedding. There were over 100 guests. Most of the guests were from my side because I had a big family, and Ann's family was quite small. Nevertheless, everyone had a good time, and it was a great wedding. Because I couldn't afford to miss too much work, our honeymoon was only one night in a hotel in Paisley, and we drove there in the work's van. Not the most romantic start to our life together!

And then it was back to Aberdeen for me. Ann continued to stay with her mum and dad in Glasgow. Now I had an even better reason to go home every weekend – to see my wife!

It was such a long journey. I would leave on Friday night after work and drive down the coast road past Stonehaven. I remember there were always lots of rabbits on the road. I know I fell asleep at the wheel at least once. Ann came up to stay a few times, and that helped.

Eventually, all the driving on top of a 40-hour week got too much, and anyway, Ann and I wanted to start our married life together properly. The only thing was, we had to decide where to live. Ann had always lived in Glasgow, so she was keen to stay there if we could. I would have loved to live in Glasgow again, but I was blacklisted, so I would never get a job. I couldn't go back. Ann, on the other hand, was a nursery nurse, so she would be able to get a job anywhere.

It became obvious that Ann had to move to Aberdeen.
We started looking for a flat together.

My pal Stevie Stewart who I had shared 2 caravans and a flat at Rosemount Place with. He was originally from Farnborough

6. ROSEMOUNT PLACE: 1980 - 1982

Another flat came up for sale, just along the street from where I was living with Steve.

Ann came to Aberdeen for the viewing. The flat had a lot going for it. It was in a good location, and there was on-street parking. Ann knew the area from the times she had come up at the weekend, and she liked it. It seemed perfect.

We arranged our first mortgage with the Leeds and Holbeck Building Society, then we put in an offer for the flat. And we got it! Our first home together.

It was a nice flat with two bedrooms, but it wasn't perfect, so I converted it to suit . It was great when it was done and perfect for entertaining! We had lots of parties. People came up from Glasgow to stay for the weekend, and we spent time out on the town, showing them the delights of Aberdeen.

Life went like a fair. It went by in a blur. Weekends flew past.

We soon made more friends in Aberdeen. One particular couple was Linda and John Patterson. He was an American, and he worked for Santa Fe Drilling. They had lots of money because oil people earned a lot at that time. They were about our age, and they had a big house in Bridge of Don and two sons.

To me, John had everything. And I wanted it, too.

I had the capability to earn money, and I was working hard, but now there was the mortgage and bills to pay, and we had spent a lot on the flat. At that time, we got paid in cash, and I never had an overdraft. I didn't really use banks much. Things could be tight, but I got lots of overtime at the weekends because there was still a shortage of engineers, and Ann was working, so we never really struggled. I had come a long way from my childhood, even then.

Scottish Gas were expanding. They built a new depot at the Links near the beach, which was very modern. Sub-contractors were given wee 'dookits' to issue work. I had my own dookit.

I was determined to get on. I showed them I had leadership qualities, and I had good ideas. This was soon rewarded. I was promoted to charge-hand and then to supervisor. There were four supervisors, and we were known as the four musketeers. We represented Maclean & Nuttall. Now I was overseeing the rest of the staff. I had grown to trust them, and my relationship with Scottish Gas got better.

Promotion had its downside, though. Now I was a supervisor I didn't get overtime. In lots of ways, it was better because it was office-based and had a salary, but I still had to pay for my own fuel and tools. To make up the difference, I took on as much extra work as I could get. Old Bob in the stores used to sell stuff at 'the back door', so I could get equipment from him for 'homers', which were cash-in-hand jobs I did after hours. When we were installing heating systems, I did the wiring myself instead of getting an electrician in, and I did the plastering when we were ripping out fireplaces. I did surveys. Anything I could get, really, that would pay.

I was working all hours, and it was beginning to make a difference to our lives.

Being a gas engineer is a big responsibility. People take gas for granted and forget how dangerous it can be. This was brought home to me one morning when I was in the depot. I heard a commotion from the radio room. The sound of sirens came over the speaker. Alarmed, I went in to find out what was going on.

I soon knew. There had been a major gas explosion at the Royal Darroch Hotel in Cults.

We had to get out there as soon as possible. All the guys were in the local cafe having breakfast, and there were no mobile phones in those days, of course. I ran round to the cafe as fast as my feet could carry me. They were surprised to see me in such a hurry. They were as shocked as I was when I explained, and we all headed out to Cults.

When we got there, it was a scene of devastation, like a bomb had gone off. There was a minibus on its roof in front of the hotel, and the remains of cars blown apart in the wreckage.

We pulled up, and we were immediately surrounded by the emergency services, vehicles and first responders. A police officer directed us into the car park opposite, and that was us for the next few days and nights. We had to stay on site so there was always a presence from the company there, sleeping where and when we could. The mood was very sombre.

Five people died in the explosion. It emphasised for me the importance of the gas engineer's job and the responsibility we had for people's lives, and I have never forgotten that.

But life and work carried on, and I was ready for my next adventure.

My mate Alex owned a pub outside Pittodrie. It was called Rocky's, after Rocky Balboa, the boxer from the film. The lower floor was a pub, with a club upstairs. He had spent a lot of money fitting it out in the latest style. All the tables were smoky glass, and there were purple Perspex phones on each table. The idea was that customers would order by phone, and the bar would deliver to the table.

He asked if I would like to work for him. I had no experience of running a pub, but I thought, *Why not?* I could work part-time, and he said I could pick my own hours. So, when I wasn't working for Maclean & Nuttall, I ran the pub during the day, pulling pints behind the bar and then the club at night. I got Ann involved too. She was on the till. I found it so easy to make a bit extra from the till in those days before electronic tills and surveillance cameras. I don't know if Ann knew I was doing it, though!

Some famous acts came to play at the club. Somehow, Alex managed to bring them in, and people would come to see them. People like Les Gray from the band Mud, and Dave Berry. I had to manage the 'green room', so I got to meet them all. The club was very successful, and we were always busy. And it gave me another chance to use my entrepreneurial skills! I used to buy produce from a couple of guys I knew who set up a market garden, and poached salmon from another guy, then I would put on a mark-up and sell it on to the club, making myself a bit of profit. I always had an eye open for new opportunities. I was working hard, and I was able to start saving for the first time.

They were good times, but they didn't last. Alex eventually got into financial difficulties. He closed the club and disappeared.

By that time, Ann and I were mostly hanging around with married couples, like Mike Maclean and his wife, Elaine. They bought a house in Bucksburn, and we used to go there for social occasions. We liked the area and decided we were going to move there, too.

All our hard work was paying off. We had come through the worst of it, and we would never know poverty again. It was time to trade up.

7. AUCHMILL ROAD - PART 1: 1982 - 1984

We moved into Auchmill Road on 1st April 1982. We had a two-bedroom terraced house on the end of a row of three. It was built on a steep hill, with the back garden higher than the front garden, and we had a walkway right around the house.

We did some internal renovations to get the house the way we wanted it. I had to lay slabs in the back, and I had to dig out a few tonnes of earth to make a flat area and put in a shed. Then, of course, we had to furnish it.

But it was great to be in a new house. We were young and on our way up in the world. Everything seemed achievable.

I had always dreamed of owning a red sports car, and now I could afford it! I bought a brand-new red Opel Manta. I thought it was really cool as it had a painted rubberised tailgate. It only had two doors and was quite a tight squeeze, especially when I was wearing my new sheepskin coat. I thought it was quite cool, but I must have looked right daft. I still didn't have any style!

So, we had all the trappings of success, including a Löwchen dog. He was a bit of a status symbol. We called him 'Frensel of Stolzenau' because of my mother-in-law, Hilde. She came from a town called Stolzenau, near Bremen. Despite being known as the 'Little Lion' dog, he was quite small. I expected him to be a bigger dog, so it was a bit embarrassing to be seen with him. We also got a cockatiel called Nikki, and he used to hang upside down on the curtains. He had some bite on him!

Then we got a lodger. Stevie Robbins was a guy from Castleford in Yorkshire, and he was looking for digs, so I thought, *Why not?* We let him have the spare room for £40 per week. We had the space, and it would be extra money for us. I was all about the money because we had a bigger mortgage now and higher bills. We had to do what we could.

I arranged for Stevie to move in one afternoon while I was at work. I came home that evening, and he opened the door to me in his pyjamas, slippers and a robe. I was gobsmacked because the distinctive rust-coloured robe he was wearing looked like mine! I thought he had overdone it in making himself at home – then I found out he had the exact same robe as me!

He stayed with us for months, until his mother became ill and he had to go home to Yorkshire. Luckily, Simon Black, one of the supervisors, made an enquiry about the room. I had fallen out with him, so I was surprised when he said he wanted a chat. But we agreed he could move in at the same rate as Stevie.

In early 1984, Ann and I took stock. Life was expensive but good. We had our own house, and we were financially stable. The time was right for the next step in our lives. We decided to start a family.

In due course, Ann became pregnant, and our first child was on the way. It was both wonderful and scary at the same time. I was going to be a father! I could only hope I would be as good a parent to my child as my father had been to me.

We needed the spare room for a nursery, so Simon had to find somewhere else to live.

Ann's pregnancy progressed, and her due date crept nearer all the time. I had planned to be there for the birth, but the baby took us all by surprise. On 29th November 1984, I was out working as usual. I knew Ann was near her due date, but I wasn't worried. I finished the job I was on and made my way back to the office, not expecting anything more exciting than finishing up and going home. Of course, they had no way to contact me while I was out of the office. As soon as I opened the door, my pal Terry Maclean ran across the room. He said, 'Ann's been taken into hospital – the baby's on the way!'

They had been anxiously waiting for me to return ever since they heard the news. I rushed to the hospital, and luckily I made it in time for the birth! It was very emotional, and I cried a lot. I will never forget how it felt to hold my firstborn, Kara, in my arms. It was a moment I wanted to last forever. I took so many pictures of my perfect little girl, but I was most impressed by her huge feet! I took a picture just of them, and I have that picture on the desk in my office to this day.

Soon, it was time to leave the hospital and take her home. It took a bit of manoeuvring to get her carrycot in the back of our red Opel Manta, and I thought, *I'm going to need a bigger car!* But it was a small price to pay.

When we got home, we placed her in her wicker Moses basket, and as I gazed down at her, I knew my life would never be the same again. I remember singing the song 'Family Man' by Hall & Oates to her as she lay there sleeping. It just seemed to fit.

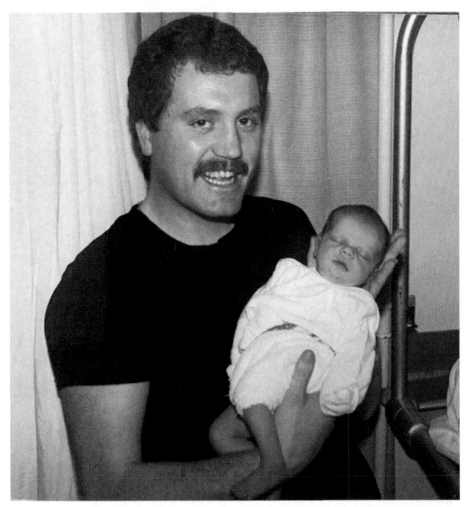

Me holding Kara shortly after she was born in 1984.

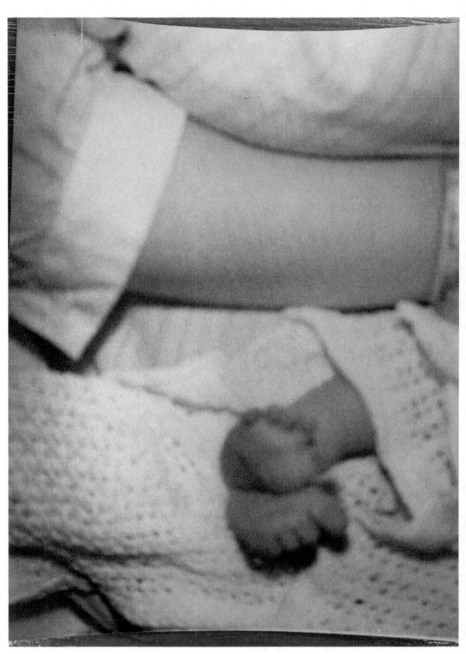

The size of Kara's feet impressed me so much I had to take this picture.

8. AUCHMILL ROAD - PART 2:
1984 - 1988

Now I had my daughter, I was even more determined to be a success. Fortunately, I was doing well in work. I had recently spent months working away from home successfully delivering contracts for the Ministry of Defence on behalf of Scottish Gas because it was too far to travel back and forth. I had missed my family, but it was worth it because I gained a lot of experience and I learned a lot. Because of those contracts, I learned how to do tenders and how to do valuations. I learned to deal with all the issues associated with contracts, rather than just overseeing the operation and the delivery of the works, and I was also getting more involved with the financial side of the business.

I had done so much to prove my worth to the company, and I had learned so much. I was being recognised by Ken Maclean and the management team for my achievements. They saw me as reliable, and I had lots of new ideas to make us look more professional. I introduced uniforms and ID cards for the engineers, and shirts and ties for supervisors. These things might seem obvious these days, but back then it was not the case, and they helped us really stand out as a modern, professional company. Just about then, we got a heating installation contract from Scottish Gas in Harthill. It was similar to the Ministry of Defence contracts, so I was appointed to run it because Ken knew I could be trusted to do a good job. All the contracts I was in charge of were run successfully and at a profit. Ken was seeing the value in my work ethic and ability and in the way I was thinking strategically and resolving issues. He wanted to expand the business, and that meant creating a new role. I was ambitious, and I was ready for promotion.

But, of course, Ken was quite pally with Simon, who had been our lodger. Simon was a funny guy, and Ken fell for his charm. He made Simon the new business development manager. I had to go along with Ken's decision, even though I wasn't very happy about it. I knew I could do the job better.

And I was right. Simon went around the country for 12 weeks or so, and he failed to generate any new work whatsoever. I told Ken I wanted to have a go, and he agreed to give me a chance.

I put out the feelers for more work right away, and it paid off. At that time, there was a government remit that meant every gas meter in the country over 20 years old had to be changed. Once Scottish Gas saw how well we were doing in the Harthill contract, they offered us the chance to do this Meter Exchange Programme. I jumped at the chance and said yes. I saw that it was a good opportunity and good long-term work, and it would be a feather in my cap if I landed it.

I worked hard on the contract, and, thinking it was sorted, I went on holiday. To my horror, when I got back, Terry, Ken's brother, had caused confusion by saying no to the contract. I was livid and had to do a quick job of reversing whatever he had said. I had to convince Scottish Gas it had been a misunderstanding and we wanted to go forward on it.

Once we sorted it out, we were quite successful. Part of the deal was that we had to provide labour for the service and maintenance side, so we opened up premises in Hyndland to support the contract. It was a dump to start with, but we made it work. We were so successful that we actually helped Davie Birrell, the Scottish Gas depot manager at Cowlairs in Springburn, and his team to win the prestigious UK-wide Silver Flame Award.

We were fast becoming recognised as an efficient, reliable contractor, and I think a lot of that was to do with the way I did things. We worked as a team, but the fact that I wanted to make everything a success helped. We certainly thought we were the best contractor in Scotland, and Scottish Gas gave us a lot of work after that. As far as Scottish Gas were concerned, it was amazing we could rise so quickly – they had never seen anything like it before. They had always struggled with contractors in the past. Now we were delivering beyond their expectations and knowing a lot of it was down to me felt good. It was simple to win work, but ultimately, you had to deliver what you said you could deliver, and we did that.

Everything was going well. I was quickly moving up the ranks in the business. The top team was me, Simon, Michael Maclean and Terry Maclean. The four of us operated across Scotland, but Ken was quickly learning that I had the most wherewithal to go out and get new work.

We went on working for Scottish Gas in Aberdeen, and we went on winning contracts. It really did prove there was work out there. Simon hadn't been successful, but I was. Of course, it was not just about success − it was also about timing and luck. But sometimes you take a chance and make your own luck.

As usual, I was always looking for new ways to turn a coin to improve my lifestyle, and I easily found other opportunities to make money. There would be scrap generated by removing old cylinders that could be sold on, and I also used to sell nearly-new electric storage heaters that had been taken out and replaced. This was extremely lucrative, particularly in Buchan and other rural areas, where people were off the main gas line and dependent on these heaters, and these were slimline heaters so they were much more aesthetically pleasing. For the cooker replacement programme, we would rock up with the new cooker and in some cases pick up and remove the old cookers. It was up to us to scrap them, but some of them would be pretty decent, and I knew I could get more for them if I tried. I had a pal, Gary Milne; he's dead now, but at that time, he had a wee second-hand shop in Aberdeen, so it made sense to sell him a few cookers every week. He got a good mark-up on them because there was a good market for them back in the day. I would also fit and test the cookers for the new owners.

All of those things brought in extra cash, and it was a good thing because money was my driving force in the early days. I would be working my regular hours during the week and working after hours and at weekends to make extra money. It was good, and things were getting better all the time.

Even with all the work, we used to have loads of fun. There was always something going on. We worked hard, and we wanted to play hard, too. On the weekend, we would play five-a-sides with the other lads and mix with the guys from Scottish Gas. Sometimes, we would even play cricket. We had lots of parties because that was one of the ways we let our hair down. A few of the lads lived in a flat, and we christened it 'Pie Capper Castle'. It was always open, and it was always party time. That was in the days when you could buy beer from pubs by the gallon. We used to frequent Gabriel's, just off Union Street in Aberdeen. They sold great Guinness, and it was the norm for a lot of us to buy gallons and take them back to Pie Capper Castle for a party after the pubs closed.

Everybody has stories to tell about that time! One time, I remember getting pretty drunk and falling asleep on the floor next to the radiator. When I woke up, I was stuck to the radiator. The heat had burned my skin onto it, and I had been too drunk to notice. The criss-cross scars stayed for months before they finally faded.

One year, we decided to throw a work's Christmas party in a small hotel in the city. At that time, Gordon Brankin was the head of Scottish Gas, and it was his wife, Ellen, and her pal who were to do the catering. That kind of thing helped to cement the ongoing relationship that we had in those days.

It was my task to collect Ellen and her pal from the suburb of Aberdeen where they lived. They were doing a buffet, and it took a couple of runs before we got all the trays of food back to the hotel. All I had to do then was take Ellen and her pal home. The weather had been atrocious, and the road was covered in snow and ice. Even though I was driving carefully, the roads were slick, and for a moment, I lost control. It was enough. Our car veered to the other side of the road, into the path of an oncoming lorry! Quickly, I swerved out of the way of the lorry and ran straight into a pole on the nearside. It sent us in a spin, and I was helpless to stop it. The car, an old Ford Cortina, spun out of control and landed in a ditch.

Every panel on the car was damaged, but we were all safe. The only damage was to Ellen – she had a broken fingernail. It was just as well. I would have been mince if I had killed the boss's wife!

We all got out of the car and stood in the snow. It was freezing! There were cars slowing down to have a look, and we could only hope someone in one of those cars would report it. Eventually, a car stopped, and it was Ellen's neighbour. He offered to take the women home, and of course, they accepted. I was left on my own. *Here we go!* I thought. It was so cold I could barely feel my fingers and toes. I was dressed for a party, not for standing around in the snow and ice!

When the police arrived, I explained what had happened. They called it in, and a pickup truck was sent from Aberdeen. As we were waiting for the truck, a car crashed into the back of another on the road right in front of us. The police decided to investigate. They found that the driver who had run into the car in front was drunk, so they arrested him and left me on my own while they took him back to the police station. So that was me. I was left standing there, still freezing, waiting to go to a party. It was an experience, that was for sure!

Eventually, I got home, got ready and got to the party. As I came in the door, there was a loud cheer! Gordon's wife had relayed the story to everybody, and I was received as a hero! It was good to be a hero because we could have all been killed, but it was only for that one night. At least I got a new car out of it!

Kara was now two years old and growing fast. Ann and I had always agreed we wanted two children, so in 1986, we decided to try again. Our second daughter, Mikaela, was born on 30th August 1987. I was there for her birth, too, and just as starstruck with Mikaela as I had been with Kara. Two daughters! Our family was complete.

Life continued to speed past. We still travelled down to Glasgow to see the family, and now we had the girls to bring along with us. Sometimes, that journey could be a bit fraught, with a toddler, a baby and Frensel the dog in the car! But 1987 was good, and I even arranged for a wee holiday break for the following summer in Blackpool.

We stayed at the Norbreck Castle Hotel, which was right on the front. It was a typical Blackpool holiday, with ice cream and donkey rides for the kids. I remember Mikaela was teething. She was really grumpy all the time and used to scream the place down wherever we went. It was a bit uncomfortable when people would look at you with the screaming baby and wonder what was going on. Kara was stung by a wasp when we were at the beachfront, and she, too, screamed the place down! Kara still doesn't like wasps to this day. But it was a great holiday. We got a beautiful drawing of Kara and Mikaela done from a photograph, and it hung on the stairwell wall at Rhindmuir Grove for years. Little did I know how things were about to change in the year to come.

Part of the Team B/Row Me, Simon Black, Steven Maclean, Ken Maclean, Mike Maclean. F/Row Derek Clifford & Terry Maclean.

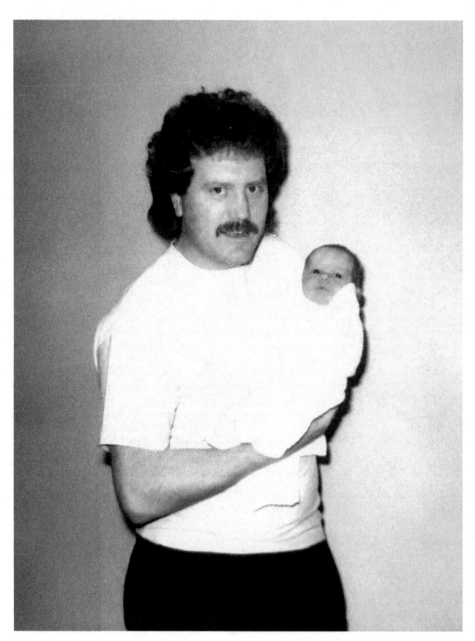

Me and Mikaela when she was born in 1987.

Kara with her Mum Ann and Mikaela.

9. AUCHMILL ROAD - PART 3: 1988 - 1990

The year 1988 was to see two major disasters that both affected Aberdeen.

The first was the Piper Alpha disaster, which happened just before Mikaela's first birthday. Piper Alpha was an oil platform in the North Sea. It produced about 10% of North Sea oil and gas. On 6th July 1988, it exploded due to a faulty safety valve, killing 165 of the men on board and two rescue workers. Only 61 men escaped.

Aberdeen was a relatively small community, and everybody was touched by this tragedy. There was a real sense of shock that such a thing had happened. The fire on the rig burned for weeks, and a specialist in oil well firefighting had to be brought in from the States to put out the burning wellheads. This was Paul Neal 'Red' Adair. He was coming to the end of a career that would see him and his team put out 2,000 oil well fires. Some people thought it would be impossible to control the oil fire on the rig, but he managed. It took him and his team nearly a month of 15-hour days to understand the fire and put it out. They eventually poured fluid into the main pipe to kill the well and poured concrete into the remaining wells to seal them permanently. He was a real hero, and you don't get many of them these days.

It was a small community in Aberdeen, and everybody knew somebody who had perished on Piper Alpha. We used to play pool in a club along the road, and one of those who died was the son of the owner. He worked behind the bar, and he had played pool with us a few times.

But fate was not finished with us yet. On 21st December, just before Christmas, PAN AM Flight 103 exploded in the skies over Lockerbie. A bomb hidden in the cargo area had detonated when the plane was at an altitude of 31,000 feet. All 243 passengers and 16 crew members were killed, as well as 11 Lockerbie residents on the ground where the wreckage landed.

It was shocking. For me as a father, it made me worry what the world was turning into, particularly because most people used planes to go on holiday and so on. Piper Alpha, you could understand, that was an accident, but Lockerbie . . . Many of the men and women who worked in Aberdeen were from England or even further afield, and they relied on aircraft to get them home and back again. Now it seemed that if you got on a plane, there was a chance you could be blown out of the skies.

The world was changing, and so was I. I had decided to become self-employed. There were several reasons for this decision. I wanted to reduce the amount of tax I was paying, and I wanted to be able to legitimately invoice jobs and bank the money. 'Homers' paid in cash, and I couldn't do anything with the money except spend it. Ann wasn't quite so supportive of this decision. I think she was worried about what might happen to our income. Trying to manage on a budget and pay bills and everything could turn out to be a bit of a challenge if our income dropped.

I discussed my decision with Ken, and we agreed that while I was self-employed, I would continue to work as a contractor with Maclean & Nuttall. It meant I would still have an income; however, I would no longer have a company car. Moira, our next door neighbour, was a policewoman, and when she heard I was looking for a car, she pointed me in the right direction. I ended up with an old police car, a Ford Granada. It still had the zips in the inner lining of the roof for the blue flashing lights. It was a big car, and it travelled well up and down to Glasgow. It was a big change from when we went down in just the Opel Manta! The four of us and the dog fitted in the new car just fine.

One day, I was heading into work when smoke started pouring out from under the bonnet. I was at the busy junction at Auchmill Road, only 300 yards from home. I jumped out and lifted the bonnet – and whoosh! The car burst into flames. All I could do was stand and watch it burn. Luckily, it happened when there was only me in the car. The consequences if the girls had been in the car with me at the time . . . it just didn't bear thinking about.

My dad was very understanding and sympathetic when I told him what had happened. He told me I could borrow his car until I got myself sorted out. It was a small Fiat Panda, and we struggled to fit everything we needed for two little girls into it, never mind ourselves. So, we went from travelling up and down to Glasgow in relative luxury to being jammed into this little car for four hours at a time. While I was very grateful, it couldn't continue for long.

In the end, I was self-employed for less than a year. I had to ask Ken to take me back on the books because I needed transport, and I couldn't afford it on my own. But it was my first taste of working for myself and running my own business, and I knew it wouldn't be the last.

My new company car was a white diesel Cavalier, the first diesel car I ever drove. The fuel made it smell quite a bit, and it took a bit of getting used to. The car itself was a good drive and very fast. I remember doing about 90 miles per hour just outside Laurencekirk. Some seagulls were pecking at roadkill. When they saw the car coming, they separated and one flew straight at me. I hit it at high speed, and the seagull was catapulted through the air and damaged the front of the grill. I had to pay to get that fixed, which was annoying, but it was a lesson. If I had been going slower, maybe that wouldn't have happened. If only that lesson had stayed with me!

I had to get it fixed because soon we would be driving to Germany for a holiday. We were going to stay with Ann's sister and her family.

Going to Germany was my first experience of driving on the wrong side of the road. We drove from Aberdeen to Harwich to catch the ferry, then drove to Stolzenau near Bremen on the Weiser River. It was quite a challenge. But it was a good experience.

What I remember most about that holiday was the food. Black breads and cheese and sticky cakes. There were lots of barbeques, and there was always beer flowing. And schnapps!

I had tried it occasionally before, but that was the first time I got a taste for it. There were different flavours, and the way they served it was different somehow.

One time, it was rabbit stew for dinner. I couldn't bring myself to eat it. That was like eating Bugs Bunny! That night, I went to bed hungry.

We tried fishing, which I'd never done before. I didn't catch anything, but it was quite exciting. I got to see the Berlin Wall, and I brought a bit home. Part of the wall was a fence, which surprised me. I had always thought it was this huge wall all the way along. The kids had a good time, but they were still little, and they would have had a good time anywhere.

Overall, it was a good holiday. And then it was time to go home and get back to normal.

But normal only lasted a short time.

On 21st April 1990, all of the family were invited to my sister Christine's house in Glasgow to celebrate her son Craig's first birthday. Everyone was there. At that time, my brother Francis lived abroad, and I was living in Aberdeen, so it was great to see them all together in one place. Mum and Dad were especially happy to see all their grandchildren.

The party was due to go on well past the girls' bedtimes, so we had arranged for Kara and Mikaela to go and stay with my mum and dad at the end of the day. That meant Ann and I could enjoy the party into the small hours. When the party was over, we would stay with Ann's parents and pick the girls up in the morning.

Mum and Dad duly went home to Brodie Road and took the girls with them. We partied on with not a care in the world. If only we had known what was to come, perhaps we would have done things differently.

The next morning, I was still in bed when the phone rang downstairs. It was for me. It was my brother Jim, who lived with my mum and dad. He was crying. And then he delivered devastating news. He told me Dad was dead.

The world changed in that moment. It would never be the same again. Instinct took over, and I asked Jim who else knew. Through his tears, he said he couldn't contact anybody. My mind worked overtime, trying to think what to do. Arthur lived near to Ann's mum and dad, so I said I would let him know.

I hung up the phone and took a deep breath. I had to tell Ann and the family what had happened, and that sense of loss, of displacement, struck me again. It didn't seem real.

Somehow, I got dressed and drove to Arthur's. I had to bang on the door to get him out of bed because he was a bit hungover from the party. I let him know what had happened. He was devastated. But I had no time to help him with his grief. I said I would meet him at Mum's, and I drove like a madman to get there. She would need my support.

When I got to the house, my mum was wailing inconsolably. Kara and Mikaela had no idea what was going on. Suddenly, their safe little world had changed, and they were just two frightened kids, glad to see their dad. I comforted them as best I could. Then I turned to Jim and asked how it had happened.

He explained Mum and Dad had been up early with the kids. Dad had said he was a bit tired and was going back to bed to have a wee lie down. About an hour later, Mum had sent Kara to see if her grandad wanted a cup of tea. Kara had come back and said she couldn't wake him. Mum went to see for herself, and she couldn't wake him either. He had suffered a heart attack and died in his sleep.

I needed to see him for myself.

I went through into the bedroom. He was lying in bed as if he were asleep. He looked so peaceful. I stood for a moment, just looking at him. I pressed my hand on his forehead. He was cold to the touch.

I couldn't stop the tears.

It was a good death, without pain, but it was a massive shock for everybody left behind. Arthur arrived soon after. When he came in, I hugged him, and that was the first time I ever hugged another man. We had experienced death before, of course, but the feeling of loss that overwhelmed us . . . This was different. This was immense.

Life was so cruel. Dad had only retired the year before. He was a man who had worked all his life, who had stayed employed while three million others in the country did not − this man's life had been a success. Yet when it was his turn to take it easy, he had been cruelly snatched away from us all at the age of only 64. It was not fair.

The whole family was overcome with grief. Dad was laid out for the viewing in an open coffin in the front bedroom, and people duly came to see him for one last time. It was unreal. How could that be my dad lying there? It was hard to accept he was gone. When the time finally came to say goodbye forever, I remember the undertaker inviting us to screw the lid on the coffin with the little brass finials. I did it willingly. It was the final thing I could do for Dad.

The funeral was surreal. The hearse took him from Brodie Road on his final journey. The mood was sombre as we walked slowly behind the hearse. It was about a mile to St Catherine's church, and I remember every single step of the way.

Some kids on bikes started cycling aggressively alongside us. We tried to ignore them, but they were persistent. Finally, one young kid got up his nerve and shouted, 'Is there a dead body inside that box?'

I was so annoyed I grabbed the boy, still sitting on his bike, and lunged him over a hedge into some garden. That shut him up. I could feel the relief of the rest of the mourners. His pals just stopped in their tracks, stunned by what I had done. Needless to say, there were no more incidents from them.

We duly arrived at the chapel. We had a beautiful service. Francis was well able to articulate how we all felt about Dad. While he was speaking, I remember feeling as if someone had touched me on the back of the neck. I was sure it was Dad, letting me know he was still there. It was weird. Later, I found out that Mary, Arthur's wife, told him that when she went to see Dad in his coffin, she saw a vision of him up near the ceiling, watching over us as we said goodbye. She swears to this day it really happened.

Following the service, we went to Lambhill Cemetery to lay Dad to rest. It was another event in my life I will never forget, watching as he was lowered into the earth for good. Mum was a bit upset that where he was buried was a new section, on a hill about 150 yards from council houses. It did look a bit bleak at the time, but over the years, trees and bushes have grown, and now it's pretty decent. We had the inscription 'Always a part of us' engraved on the headstone. We thought that was a fitting epitaph because it was the truth.

Not a day goes by that I don't think of him, and I'm sure all my brothers and sisters are the same. We always try to do something together on the anniversary of his death or his birthday. It's just something we do to commemorate him, and I will always be grateful he was in my life.

10. BINNIEHILL ROAD / CALDERWOOD GARDENS - PART 1: 1990

One of the biggest regrets of my life is that I never told my dad I loved him. I had left home in 1979 to work in Aberdeen on a six-week contract, and except for weekends, I had never returned. It was now 1990. I had been too busy trying to do well and get on in life that I forgot to spend enough time with Mum and Dad. I made sure from that day on to always tell my mum that I loved her. I didn't want to make the same mistake twice.

Now she was on her own, the family were rallying round. I wanted to be part of that. I wanted to spend more time with her. I had always known I would return to Glasgow someday, and now the time had come.

The property market in Aberdeen at that time was quite flat, but we put our house up for sale even though we had nowhere of our own to go to. The driving force was to get back to Glasgow, and nothing else mattered. We eventually sold the house on 27th September 1990, less than six months after Dad had died. We got less for it than we had hoped, but it didn't matter. We were going home.

I was quite emotional when I locked the door for the last time. I stood and thought about all the good times we had had there and all the friends who had come through that door. I remembered bringing first Kara and then Mikaela home from the hospital and watching them grow from babies into little girls with personalities and minds of their own. This house was the only home they had known, and now I was taking them away from it. I could only hope they would come to love Glasgow just as much.

We were moving to Binniehill Road in Cumbernauld. Francis had bought a new house there, and he agreed we could stay in the house on the basis that I snagged it out with the builder. That was fine by me. At least it gave us a roof over our heads.

While we were looking for a house of our own, we split our time between Binniehill Road and Calderwood Gardens in Baillieston, which was Ann's mum and dad's house. This was the area we wanted to move into, so this allowed us to register at the doctor's surgery and to register the girls at St Bridget's school. Moving from Aberdeen to Glasgow was quite traumatic for the girls because they had to leave all their pals behind. It was a big thing, so we wanted to make sure they weren't messed about too much. Sometimes they would stay with their gran and grandad to make the school run easier. We soon settled in and got into a routine. We had no choice – we just had to make the most of it.

At work, everything was going well in and around the west coast. We had all the business Scottish Gas had given us, and things were a bit easier for me because I was no longer travelling up and down from Aberdeen. That made a big difference.

The wee offices and stores in Hyndland were a bit out of the way, and as the work continued to grow, we realised we needed new premises. We started to look around, and eventually, we settled on a place in Tabernacle Lane in Cambuslang that had a yard and parking and all the offices and facilities we needed. When we relocated there, it felt like we were going places. The contracts were performing well, and everything was on the up.

But nothing was happening on the house-hunting side. It was crazy. We kept putting in offers and being rejected, and we lost money every time. It was very frustrating. Then one day, I saw an advert in the *Daily Record* newspaper for a company called Glasgow Homesmith. They were looking for people to take part in a self-build project in Swinton. That was a nice part of the extended Baillieston area, within the locality where we wanted to be. I called them to arrange a meeting, and I went along to find out more about it. At that meeting, I met Bill Barclay, Eddie Docherty and Dennis, who was the site foreman.

The aim of the project was to build 24 houses, and the idea was that a crowd of people with different skill sets would commit to doing so many hours per week free of charge to get a less expensive house each at the end of it.

The land had already been purchased. It was a four-acre site near the kennels in Swinton, and all the planning was in place. It sounded like a good idea. I asked a lot of questions, and they wanted to know my background and my skill set to see if I would fit in. When I explained what I was and how I was involved in heating and gas and plumbing, they wanted me to sign up there and then. I said I would go home and think about it and let them know as soon as I had made a decision. It was a big commitment, especially since I was trying to grow Maclean & Nuttall. However, after some thought, I decided to do it.

When I signed up, I insisted on getting a particular plot. I could tell that the finished house would be great. It would be spacious and sizeable, and we would make money on it if and when we sold it on. That, of course, was a big driver for me. I wanted a decent return on the investment of my time and expertise! Little did I know this project was to be a major part of my life for the next two years and beyond.

We had to take four acres of green site and turn it into a beautiful housing estate. What a challenge! It was really exciting, but I had to try to fit it in around my normal work, which was becoming extremely busy. We had moved into Tabernacle Lane, and operational activities were growing. It meant I was working all hours of the day and night to keep everything going. That included making sure we had the right staff.

When we moved to Tabernacle Lane, the girl in the office decided to leave, so we arranged interviews for her replacement. The interviews were pretty mundane. I wasn't really keen on any of them, and I began to think we would have to settle for the best of a bad bunch.

And then in walked Mary.

Mary was like a breath of fresh air. She reminded me of the nurse who looked after me when I had my tonsils out, and my teacher, Mrs O'Hare. I liked her right away. The interview went very well and Mary was just what we were looking for. She was offered the job on the spot, and she accepted. She could start right away.

That was a decision that would eventually change my life.

Shortly after Mary was hired, we got the opportunity to tender for some warm air replacements. If we were successful, it would be our first work in Scotland outside Scottish Gas. This was an opportunity to strike out on our own and build the business without relying on Scottish Gas.

It was for three blocks of flats in Clydebank, and Terry and I went to survey them. We knew we could do the work, and we put a bid together. It was just a case of getting Ken's approval because he didn't want to upset Scottish Gas. He had over 100 men working for them, and they were still our biggest employer. However, when I advised him Scottish Gas were not bidding (even though I knew they were) he agreed we should submit the bid, so we did.

The bid was successful, and we won the work. Terry and I were cock-a-hoop. The company was actually on a contract of its own, and it was a good feeling. That particular contract went on to be our most successful ever and was a catalyst for change in the business because Scottish Gas were furious when they found out. The backlash was swift and costly. They started reducing the number of operatives we supplied to them. Ken was worried he would lose a lot of his revenue stream, but I tried to reassure him. I told him we should see it as an opportunity to expand and compete against Scottish Gas. Why should we go through them when we were just as capable? And besides, I had a personal stake in all this.

I am not one to hold a grudge, but I never forgot how Scottish Gas had sacked me when I was a young lad. Revenge is a dish best served cold, as far as I am concerned.

As the workload with Scottish Gas waned, it made us more determined to compete against them. Our next opportunity was Inverclyde Council, which we successfully won, taking it off Scottish Gas, who were the incumbent. It was for 6,500 properties down on the west coast. We were on a roll. I could almost taste our success.

However, Inverclyde was too far away to support from the Glasgow premises. We would have to set up a local office. By this time, Mary was indispensable to the business, so she was a natural choice to travel up and down to Inverclyde with me to get the new office set up.

It meant we spent a lot of time travelling together, and on the long journeys, we gradually began to find out more about each other. I told her about my dad and she opened up to me about some of her private life. Like me, she had two daughters, Vicki and Linzi who were roughly the same ages as Kara and Mikaela, so we had that in common. Mutual respect grew between us, and we became good friends.

She would sometimes go to Vic's Bakery for sandwiches at lunchtime, and one day she asked me if I wanted one, so I said, 'Yeah.'

She brought back a prawn sandwich, which I hate. I was upset, and I gave her a hard time for not knowing I didn't like prawn sandwiches! We still talk about it to this day.

When she was going for the sandwiches, I used to give her a £100 note, just to prank her and also to try to impress her, but she would always pay. Over the years, she has always paid her way.

11. BINNIEHILL ROAD / CALDERWOOD GARDENS - PART 2: 1991

The business was going from strength to strength. We won the contract for Cumbernauld and Kilsyth, which was about 4,000 properties, and we also won quite a few housing association contracts. And my contribution to the growth of the business was recognised. Ken organised a management meeting in a big hotel by Lake Windermere. I was presented with the 'Manager of the Year' award, and I got a £1,000 bonus and a gold statuette. That would be the first of many awards, and I was proud of what I had achieved, even though I had always known I would be a success.

It was especially nice to be recognised as a success at Maclean & Nuttall since I was effectively doing two jobs. I was working for Maclean & Nuttall during the day, and at night and weekends, I was working on the houses.

I got everyone I knew involved, as long as they were useful. One of the neighbours at Binniehill Road, Gerry Cox, was a plumber, a good hard worker, so I got him involved in the project. I also got my sister Christine and her husband, Raymond, involved. He worked for ADT, so he was able to put in the alarms. My brother Francis lived abroad, but I got him involved because he had money to spare. I told him it was a good investment, and he took me up on it. At the end of the build, one of the houses would be his.

At the building site, we had established a compound and had the two roads and the hammerheads in, so we had started to make some progress. There was a right old mix of people involved. We had some people who obviously had trades skills, but there were a lot of people who didn't have any technical skills but might know something about accountancy and such like, which would also be useful, and in the meantime, they could do stuff like labouring and putting up fences. At first, everybody was committed to the project, or so it seemed. However, that would change.

The first thing we had to do was lay out the strip foundations. I remember we did this on Christmas week. Me, Bill, Eddie and Dennis were all pushing concrete around the foundations while everybody else was too busy getting on with Christmas shopping. It was then I knew there would be trouble ahead.

We had run-ins with brickies for fitting bricks upside down and Monoblock layers for using the wrong sort of blocks. We nearly came to blows sometimes, but time was money, so we ended up spending all sorts of hours on site, and we would do anything to save money. Once, I think we buried a dumper truck and said it had been stolen so we could get a new one on the insurance. And there were a few tricks some of the guys knew from working on building sites. If we were short of pavings or cornerstones, Big Bill and I would don our high-viz jackets and go and dig them up from the building site up the road.

Wimpey opened a site next to us, and Bill and I had an idea. One night, we stayed on late. When we thought it was safe, we cut a hole in the fence and used our two big dumpers to run back and forward, dumping our spoil on the Wimpey site instead of paying to get rid of it. It was a misty night, and it was quite eerie. Suddenly, blue flashing lights appeared through the mist. It was the police. They had had complaints from some of the neighbours about the noise. The police told us to stop, but we also didn't want to fall out with the neighbours, so we did as we were told.

There were lots of light-hearted moments, of course, especially in the early days. We used to feed a squirrel and used to joke about it becoming diabetic from all the chocolate biscuits. Then there was the time a lad came up to the compound selling stolen rugs. Me and Bill gave him the option of being given up to the police or having the rugs confiscated. He took the latter option, and we let him go. Later, we sold the rugs on to the other members and kept a few for ourselves.

However, as time went on, the dynamic changed as it became obvious that some people were more interested in their own needs than the group needs. Ultimately, it was me, Bill, Eddie, Gerry and Dennis who got control of the group.

There was a monthly evaluation with the bank, and if we had met our targets, the bank would release funds. But that didn't always happen, and we had to make up the shortfall. There were times I had to pay wages to brickies and the like from my own pocket because the drawdown wasn't coming as fast as it should. People were dropping out of the scheme all the time, for all sorts of reasons. And some of them took it hard. It was strange to see so many grown men cry because their dream was over.

We tried to get other people involved to keep up the momentum, but that didn't always happen. It meant we had to employ more subcontractors to keep the work going apace. Eventually, I took over the costs associated with the remaining houses because there was nobody else available to take them over. It was very costly, but I knew it would pay dividends in the long run. I saw it as an opportunity to make money, and I was always up for that.

It was intense, but despite all the problems, we were making good progress. We were the core team, and we kept pushing to make it all work. I was involved in every aspect, from roofing to laying tiles, and we were always trying to save money, so we would turn our hands to anything. We were in charge of the site, and with that came responsibility. But it also gave us some perks. For instance, we were able to get a system boiler instead of the combi-boilers the others were getting, and Bill and I added chimneys to our buildings at no extra cost to us. We could do it, so we thought, *Why not?*

We also extended the size of our gardens. It was almost like payment for all our extra involvement, and we did all right out of it.

The first houses were completed, and people started to move into them. That led to some squabbles. Obviously, the people that were moving into the houses started concentrating on their own houses instead of helping across the board. That was very selfish because we needed everybody on board to get it completed as soon as possible.

We pushed on, and eventually, all the houses were up. The drop-out rate was so high by then that we ended up having to sell off some of the houses. That was quite successful, but in the end, we were left with two unsold properties. I took them on myself, and I ended up having to pay all the costs associated with them. It cost me a bit of money, but I looked on it as a long-term investment. I knew I would eventually sell and make some money out of them. When I did sell, I made about £30,000 profit on each of them, which was pretty good.

I remember walking out of the solicitors with the surplus cash in lump sums, which you could do in those days. I flashed the notes in front of Mary, trying to impress her, but I don't think it worked!

Me and Bill fitting a chimney pot on the house at Rhindmuir Grove.

Me with Kara and Mikaela inspecting progress on our new home at Rhindmuir Grove.

Me teaching Kara to drive the Dumper whilst Mikaela looks on.

12. RHINDMUIR GROVE - PART 1: 1991 - 1993

Our house got its habitation certificate, and that allowed us to finally move in. Despite the excitement, there was still a lot to do. The house was habitable according to building control, but that didn't mean it was finished. While there was running water and so on, it was all pretty basic. But the girls now had a room each, so they were pretty excited about that and it made me smile to see them.

However, we were living on a building site. We were surrounded by incomplete houses, scaffolding and piles of earth. There were no proper roads or streetlights, and it was a bit bleak. But we were now in this house that was going to become our home, and we were determined to make it work.

We eventually concluded the formal purchase of the house on 12th December 1991. Two weeks later, we woke up to our first Christmas in Rhindmuir Grove. Although it was less than perfect, I hoped that Christmas morning would be the first of many very happy memories we would create in this house I had virtually built with my own two hands to make a home for my family. It was something special, and I felt a warm glow at the thought, even if we had to go to Ann's parents' house for dinner because we didn't have any proper furniture.

I was proud of everything I had achieved that year, building the business as well as building houses.

And then it was 1992. That year was really the start of it for the business. We won two contracts in quick succession. Scottish Gas was on the wane, and the whole year flew past. We were growing the business exponentially on the west coast as well as winning work in all other areas in Scotland. Scottish Gas had reduced our manpower in all contracts, but we still had a good number of guys in Aberdeen, which always was, and continues to be, a difficult place to get resources. The company was growing, and our name for delivering a good service was spreading

Then one day, Ken called me and told me we would be getting visitors from Schlumberger Industries. I had never heard of them, but I soon found out they were one of the biggest firms in the oil exploration sector and were a global company. Apparently, they were interested in buying Maclean & Nuttall. I wasn't sure how to feel about this, but I decided to keep an open mind.

Tony Hadley, who was the operational director, and Dave Evans, the finance director, came to visit and assess the company. Ken told us he wanted the office to appear busy on the day, so I arranged for the guys to ring us up on the phones to make the place look busier than normal!

Tony and Dave were well-presented and clever. It was a bit intimidating, but later we got some good feedback. They had been impressed. I wondered what this would mean for the company and for my future, but I soon put it to the back of my mind because Ken was heading to Ireland for a few days, and he had left me to finalise a bid for Glasgow City Council. It was for service and maintenance as well as the heating works for 79,000 properties. I submitted the bid and hoped for the best.

A few weeks later, Terry and I were driving back to Tabernacle Lane when I got a call in the car. I was one of the first people to have a car phone, and I was quite proud of it. In those days, the phone was attached to the car, not truly mobile like phones are now. I pulled over to take the call. It was Andy from Glasgow City Council. He told us we had won the contract.

This was huge. This was the biggest social housing contract in Scotland. One of the biggest in the UK. And we had just taken it from the incumbent – which was Scottish Gas. This was something different. There was a definite shift happening in the industry. Here we were, a Liverpool-based contractor winning work from Scottish Gas. Full of excitement, I called Ken to let him know. He could hardly believe it. Neither could I!

And then the panic set in. For a contract this size, we would need new premises, more staff, a fleet . . . And we would have to get it done quickly because the start date was frighteningly close.

Terry and I got on to the search for premises right away, and we found a big warehouse and offices at Dykehead Street in Queenslie. It was very run down, but it had more space. We submitted a bid in excess of the offer price, but it failed. We were desperate to get it sorted as the contract was coming at us in the next few months, and we had to get everything set up. Luck smiled upon us. A couple of weeks later, the solicitor selling the premises at Dykehead Street called back. Apparently the preferred bidder had pulled out, and he was asking if we were still interested. Ken was unavailable, so I made an executive decision. I called the solicitor back and offered him a price that was £20,000 lower than our original bid. The offer was accepted.

I was cock-a-hoop. I'd pulled off a great deal and saved the company £20,000. Ken was delighted, but he never gave me a bonus or any recognition of the £20,000 I'd saved him!

So, we cracked on. It meant a complete reconstruction of the new premises as well as getting infrastructure and communications and all that sort of stuff set up. It was absolutely manic. I used the skill set I'd gained building houses to put our new office complex in place as fast as possible.

We also had to get staff. Terry had to find engineers. Mary had to set up interviews for office staff at the local job centre in Easterhouse.

Then we needed a fleet of vehicles. The only thing we could get in volume were Citroens. These were horrible wee vans, but we had to take them. We got them done in the red livery of the company, and soon they became known as the 'red devils'.

We were ready to go!

13. RHINDMUIR GROVE - PART 2: 1993 - 1995

The day came for the start of the contract. We had a brand-new office, with all the furniture and equipment we needed and all the staff and engineers. We had radio systems in all the vans so we could keep in contact with the engineers and a radio controller to run it. Everything was new and shiny, and there was a real buzz about the place.

The contract kicked off on time, and it was as successful as it could be. We were now in the big league. We had done nothing on this scale before. It was crazy and very busy. We were learning as we went along – learning to be the best we could be. We were all working all hours, and the offices were manned 24/7 because we had to accommodate the out-of-hours emergency calls. This was a new thing for us. I found it hard to finish at a certain time because I was always getting involved and drawn into things, and so were Terry and Mary. There were always people milling about late at night. It was a bit manic, but it was good. Sometimes, at night, me and the gang would be out in the city, and we would see all these red Maclean & Nuttall vans out and about. We'd actually created that, and it was a good feeling.

We wanted to create a real team dynamic, so we would have staff nights where we would buy a load of Chinese meals from Young's Kitchen in Baillieston and have karaoke in the main office. It was the only time I've ever done karaoke – I wasn't very good! I would gladly have never done it again. But it was worth it to build the team.

Everyone was involved. Even our girls – Kara, Vicki, Linzi and Mikaela – used to come into the office on the weekends when it was quieter. The girls all became good pals, and they spent some weekends together at Mary's caravan. They even christened it KelDon, a mixture of all our surnames. It was great to see them getting on so well. Mary and I were so much a part of each other's lives that I could not imagine life without her.

With everything going on, there wasn't much time for family holidays, but we did go to Limassol in Cyprus in 1993. That was a great holiday, and we all loved it. Part of it was a three-day trip to Egypt. I remember sailing into Port Said and disembarking and hearing this loud Scottish voice. It was from a guy called 'McGregor the Beggar'. He was a 'looky-looky' man. He was selling fake Rolex watches, which later in life I would buy many.....real ones of course but he had got the Scottish accent spot on to attract the tourists.

We travelled to Cairo in a coach, driving on a single-track road through fields where people were living in sheds or tents. It was one of my first experiences of real poverty. I didn't like it. We had been poor as children, but we always had a roof over our heads and enough food to eat.

Cairo itself was a bustling city. At that time, it had about eight million people living in the city, and another eight million would descend on it during the day. It was absolutely mental. There were buses with hundreds of people on them, sitting on the top, hanging off the sides, like it was on TV . . . It was a wonder there was never a major accident. But it just seemed to be typical for them.

We went to the museum to see the mask of Tutankhamun and to a papyrus factory where we got scrolls made up for each of us with our names done in hieroglyphics. That was quite cute, and I think we've still got them tucked away somewhere. Our next stop was the pyramids and the Sphinx. It was very, very strange going from an overcrowded city to suddenly being on the edge of the desert. We got a horse and cart to take us up to the actual pyramids, and we actually went down into Khufu's sarcophagus. That was really fascinating. The kids loved it. It was a great adventure for them, and they still talk about it to this day. It was a great holiday.

And then it was home and back to work. The big contract was going well, and it started to feel like the company was going places. Little did we know it was all about to change yet again.

In the background, Ken had continued his talks with Schlumberger, and they had come to a conclusion. In January 1994, Maclean & Nuttall was sold to Schlumberger.

It was strange. I'd worked for Ken since 1979. It had been effectively a family business, and now we were suddenly part of a corporate company. The ground that had been solid under my feet was starting to shift. I had no idea what it would mean for me. I was worried there might be changes, but we were told to keep doing everything the same way until we were told to do something different. So that was what we did. We continued as normal.

In the meantime, I had diversified into another area – being an extra in the movies! My brother Arthur worked with Lee Lighting, and he was heavily involved with the production of TV programmes, like *Taggart* and *Still Game,* as well as movies. He had been the 'best boy' on the movie *Shallow Grave,* a kind of black comedy murder movie, and some of my brothers and sisters had been involved in the TV shows.

I found this very interesting, and I asked him if there was anything I could get involved in. I could just see myself in front of the camera! He eventually got back to me and said they were doing a movie about drugs, and it was based on a book called *Trainspotting.* Was I interested?

I jumped at the chance. I would be paid £50 per day, and that sounded all right to me. When I signed up a few days later, I was told to report to the old George Hotel at the top of Buchanan Street in Glasgow. Not knowing what to expect, I went in and almost immediately bumped into Ewan McGregor, the star of the film, who was already in character as Renton. It was very strange. My brother introduced me to the producer, Danny Boyle, who seemed like a nice chap.

Then I was left with the coordinator, who would look after me and tell me what was to happen. The first thing was to go to the costume department. Apparently, I was to be a policeman, but none of the uniforms fitted me. So, instead, I was used for other, non-specific roles. There was one disco scene where we had to dress up in glad rags and strange, sparkly outfits. It was midday, and there was no alcohol! It was very strange to be dancing with complete strangers and pretending to be enjoying ourselves. It was a good laugh but very surreal. We had to do that scene several times, and there were special effects added, so by the end of it, I couldn't be made out. Which was just as well because I was no John Travolta!

I was in another scene where Renton's mum goes to bingo, and she actually wins. You hear her shouting out. Then it goes into a speeded-up special effect, then it pans to a dejected bingo player who lost – and that was me! I'm on screen for a whole second. That's my claim to fame!

It was a great experience. It took about two weeks for my parts to be done. There was lots of hanging about, but I got paid and there were yummy à la carte meals from the food wagon you could help yourself to. And there were lots of snacks. It was good to mix with lots of new people, some of them famous and some not so famous. Obviously, Ewan McGregor and all of the cast went on to worldwide fame, as did Danny Boyle. For me, it was all about trying to get a bit of extra money.

My acting career didn't go much further, though my brother did arrange for me to go on the set of the movie *Rob Roy*. The stars were Liam Neeson and Tim Roth, and when I was there, they were playing a scene near the end of the film where there is a sword fight that Rob Roy wins. It was very exciting to be on set for what turned out to be such an iconic scene. I got to meet Liam Neeson, and it struck me how tall he was. I am tall myself, and he seemed to tower over me in his costume with his kilt and big sword. I also got to see the models that were used on set, based on the villages at night-time. I spent the whole day there, and it was good fun, a good memory.

At work, Mary and I still spent quite a lot of time together because of the job, and sometimes we would go for lunch to the Garfield Hotel or maybe a Chinese restaurant. We got on well, and it was good to spend time together. It made life easier for both of us. If she needed stuff done on her house or caravan, I would try to help out because we had access to all the tradesmen. It was that sort of relationship. We were good pals.

I doubt the business would have been as successful without Mary. She had a big impact on creating the systems and putting the processes in place and ensuring we got some good people in there. I remember Terry Maclean saying to me that I was only good because I had Mary. Big Bill, who was a bit of a character, used to pop into the office every now and then to see how things were. He would refer to us as 'Beauty and the Beast'. He thought it was funny, and maybe it was.

When we won a million-pound contract for West Dumbarton that took us up to 120,000 properties, it was reported all the way back up to Schlumberger headquarters in Paris and New York, and I got all the plaudits for it. It was a big contract for those days, and there was a big fuss made about it. As the team from Schlumberger started to get their feet under the table and understand who did what, it became clear to them that while Terry was the regional manager and I was the area manager, it was me who had a lot of the ideas and I made things happen.

Everything seemed to be going well, at least for me. But the same could not be said for Ken. Not long after he sold the business, his wife, Jean, died of cancer. Of course, I had known Jean for many years, and the funeral was a very sad occasion.

Ken stepped back from the business at that time. But the rest of us stepped up. We were invited to attend several management meetings in London and even Paris on occasion. That was the way Schlumberger liked to do things. They liked to get people involved and sitting round a table together. It just cost the business money, and that wasn't the way we were used to doing things – but, of course, it was up to them. It was their business now.

We saw it as a free trip to London or Paris, so we were determined to have a good time. I remember, one time, Dave Hutchison, Mary and I went to Paris. After the business of the day was done, we hit the town. We all had a good time exploring the bars of the famous city – especially Dave! The next morning, we went for a walk to clear our heads. The weather was lovely, and we enjoyed wandering around for a while. Dave was feeling a bit under the weather, so we stopped for a rest. He lay down on the grass in the sun and fell asleep. That was clearly not permitted, and a big gendarme came over to move him on. He was still a bit drunk, and the gendarme had to kick him a few times to wake him up. The look on his face was a picture! Mary and I laughed our socks off. Those were good times, and we always had a laugh.

Eventually, Schlumberger decided to spend more time in the Glasgow office. The ways of working were beginning to change, and we were having to do monthly management reports and work in a more professional way. The culture of a PLC was totally different from a private company. But we just played the game and did what we were told. When they finally produced a set of accounts, it showed a loss.

They asked, 'How did we make a loss?'

And I responded, 'Well, because we're doing it your way. When we did it our way, we always made a profit!'

Working for Ken had been fairly relaxed, and I had a lot of autonomy. Now things were slowly but surely changing. It made me unsettled, and I wasn't alone.

Terry made it clear that he had no time for the Schlumberger guys and was often quite rude to them. Of course, I took advantage and asked for more money and a new car, which I got. They also decided to split Terry's role into two. I was promoted to regional manager for the west coast, and Terry became regional manager for the east coast. The restructure didn't go down well with Terry, and ultimately, he got to the stage where he had enough. In early 1996, he left and set up his own business, Gas Care Scotland.

This was only one of many changes. Mary also felt undervalued and wanted to leave the business. I wasn't happy about this. Mary and I were a team. We had been on a journey together. It was down to us that the business was in the position it was. Besides, I would miss her. She was so much a part of my everyday life, I had no idea how I would manage without her.

We had this idea that we might start a business together. We discussed it for a while and decided to go ahead and set it up so it would be there for us if we ever decided to make our idea a reality. The result was Gas Call Services, which I formed in February 1996. The name came to me while I was in the Clachan Bar in Garrowhill with my brother Arthur. I told him I was going to set up a business and I needed the right name. For some reason, I had the *Ghostbusters* theme song in my head, and it came out as, 'Who you gonna call? Call Gas Call!' That was how the name came about.

That night in the Clachan, I told Arthur, 'One day I will employ 100 men.'

I'm not sure if he believed me, but I knew if I put my mind to it, I could make Gas Call a success. It wouldn't happen overnight, of course. I knew it would take a few years, but I was determined to make my prediction come true.

Me and my moment of fame in a scene from the movie Trainspotting.

It is surreal how the Great Pyramids of Giza sit right on the edge of Cairo.

*Kara, Mikaela and Ann coming back up and out of Khufu's sarcophagus in the
Great Pyramid.*

14. RHINDMUIR GROVE - PART 3: 1995 - 1996

Despite my best attempts to persuade her otherwise, Mary decided to leave the company. It was a big change for me. Mary had been by my side for many years, and she had been instrumental in the growth of Maclean & Nuttall. The office just wasn't the same without her. I missed our cups of tea and the laughs we had.

All of these changes were making me unsettled. After Mary and Terry left the business, I wanted to tender my resignation. I did it several times, but Tony Hadley kept talking me out of it. It was a very anxious time.

And then, after 15 years of marriage, Ann and I decided to separate.

Ann had worked as a nursery nurse right up until we had Kara because we needed two salaries to pay the mortgage and everything. After Kara was born, she gave up work outside the home and took up the roles of housewife and mother. I think in the early days, she was quite supportive of me working long hours and travelling about the country. It was a means to an end, and while I was earning, we could afford things, which was good. I was always good at providing. But after 15 years, enough was enough for both of us. At that time, it was really busy at work, and I was spending most of my time there. That certainly contributed to the break-up.

I bought Ann out of the house and gave her a lump sum and a car and some other bits and pieces. We split everything. Ann took the girls and went back to live in Aberdeen. It was a hard time for everybody, especially Kara and Mikaela, but I took the view it was better to have two happy homes than one miserable one. I missed them a lot, and I made an effort to see them every other weekend. The house was so quiet without them. They would either come down to Glasgow, or I would go to Aberdeen. Back to travelling that road again! But it was worth it to see my girls and spend time with them.

After I split up with Ann, I was going through some issues. Mary would sometimes invite me over to her place for dinner, which was very nice and considerate of her. I got to know her family a lot better, and it was nice to get out of my own empty house for a while. Mary and I had got on well at work. We were a bit of a team. Now I was becoming part of her family. I was helping them out with stuff like repairs to the house and caravan, but they were helping me and it all seemed to be quite good. Both families even went on holiday together to Ibiza.

It was turning out to be a very challenging year, and it wasn't over yet. One night, I got home very late from work. It had been busy at the office that day, and I just wanted to rest. The night was extremely cold, and as I got home, I could see a big, thick slab of ice in front of the door. I didn't think much of it, but when I opened the door, I was horrified. The upper stairwell above the staircase had fallen down, and I could hear running water. The house was flooded.

The water was so deep it was coming out of the front door, and that had made the ice. I waded into the kitchen to turn off the water. It was freezing cold, and my legs were numb by the time I did it. But the damage was done. I looked around me, and my heart sank. There were huge sheets of icicles above the back door where water was running out over the ceiling and out of the soffits. That shows how cold it was.

It turned out the main pipe above the bathroom had burst. It was only a short piece of pipe, but it had frozen and split, causing extensive damage.

The next day, I got in touch with the insurance company, and they told me they would send out an assessor. In the meantime, I had to throw all my soaking clothes and bedding and everything into the garage. Mary and I put lists together to get estimates, and that was all very helpful. Little did I know it would take months to sort out. There was building work to be done, and the place had to be put back together. It was a nightmare.

The claim came out at about £70,000. That reflected the amount of damage done. It was a bit strange because even after I had settled, there would be times when I found water in light bulbs! It had dripped through the ceiling and into the light bulbs. They were still working, which was bizarre. I don't know how the assessor missed it.

It was a very strange time, and it just added to the anxiety and the trauma of what was quite a challenging year.

To add insult to injury, I was caught speeding for a third time in a relatively short period.

The first time was near West Dumbarton, and the second was near Falkirk. I had six points on my licence, and I really should have been paying more attention to my driving. I was on my way back from Aberdeen. I had been to visit Kara and Mikaela, and I was rushing because we had a big tender to go in. I was in a big car, and I was firing down the road thinking about other things, particularly the tender. Suddenly, I spotted this blue flashing light in my rearview mirror. My blood ran cold. I pulled over, and the police car pulled in behind me. My heart was in my mouth as I watched the police officer walk up to the car. It turned out I had been doing 111 miles per hour. I was breathalysed as a matter of routine. It was negative, of course, but the big copper sent me on my way with a warning that anything over 100 was usually an automatic ban.

I was very remorseful, but it was too late. I wondered what I was going to do because if I lost my licence, anything could happen. How would I see Kara and Mikaela? I could even lose my job. I was terrified. If I wasn't able to earn, I wouldn't be able to pay maintenance money for the girls.

I duly received a court summons, and I had to appear at Arbroath Sheriff Court. I asked Mary to go with me in case I lost my licence so she could drive me back. We had to be at the court for nine o'clock, so we left early.

What a day that was. It turned out that because I had no representation, the judge had pushed me to the back of the queue. We sat through a load of cases and watched people being banned. I was sure it would happen to me. We were the last called. The judge gave me a telling-off for having no representation. I said, 'Look, nobody advised me of that. I didn't realise I needed it.'

He agreed to let me represent myself, and I explained about the separation and things that were going on at work. I pleaded with him to let me keep my licence or I would not be able to see Kara and Mikaela.

He must have taken pity on me because he fined me £750 and added five points to my licence, making it 11 points, one point short of the 12 that would have meant a ban. I thanked the judge, and we high-tailed it out before he had a chance to change his mind. Apparently, it was the first time he hadn't banned someone for doing over 100 miles per hour. I was very thankful for that.

It was obvious I had been working too hard and everything was finally catching up with me. I decided it was finally time for me to leave Maclean & Nuttall. So much had changed since the acquisition of the business by Schlumberger in 1994. It wasn't the same place. The culture was totally different. I missed Terry and Mary, and I no longer felt I had a future with the company.

It had been a journey to get here from where I started, and I had learned so much. I had travelled up and down the UK and experienced many roles, from being an original gas engineer 'on the tools' to the heights of regional manager. I had learned to do presentations and how to tender and win work. I had also learned how to deliver a service and make a profit as well as keeping clients happy. Eighteen years of experience with the same company – it was quite an achievement! But now it had become only a stepping-stone for the next part of my journey.

I advised Tony Hadley of my decision. He told me they couldn't just keep accepting my resignation requests. I told him it was finally happening, and what's more, I would be taking them to a tribunal for messing me about.

I was leaving, and I wanted to get something back. I suggested they had failed to provide me with appropriate training for my new role. His jaw nearly hit the floor when he realised I was serious. I stood my ground. At that point, Maclean & Nuttall had about 1,100 employees and were the biggest gas company outside of British Gas. That was quite an achievement, and I had helped to make it happen. And suddenly, I was being put in a position where I felt I was forced to leave. I needed some compensation.

Ultimately, I was put on garden leave. I received tens of thousands of pounds and the use of my company car for six months. I was relatively happy with this, and I remember Tony asked me what I was going to do. I told him I would be taking a break and then setting up my own business.

He was quick to suggest I should take a long break and suggested using the money I had received for a gap year, to travel and see the world. I told him I would decide. I never saw him after that, but I'm still in touch with him through 'LinkedIn'. I liked Tony. He taught me a lot. He was a gifted academic, and he said things back then that have stuck with me to this day. He really was a clever guy.

I finally left Maclean & Nuttall in late 1996. It was a strange feeling after all those years, but there was a sense of relief, too. The next part would be up to me.

15. RHINDMUIR GROVE - PART 4: 1996 - 1997

I was effectively unemployed, but I had plenty to keep me busy. I was still trying to get the house back in shape after the flood, and I had the use of the company car and fuel card. I was 39, living on my own in a big house with a fair bit of money in the bank. I could have sat back and relaxed for a while. But it was not the time to rest on my laurels. It was always in the back of my mind that my income had stopped, and I had to pay the bills and child support every month.

I decided to invest £10,000 in Gas Call Services. It was a bit of a gamble, but I was relatively comfortable with it. I had been working, and I had been living on my own since Ann and the kids left. I would be quite secure financially, at least for a while. I opened up a bank account with the Clydesdale Bank and deposited the £10,000. That was the start of it all.

It felt good. There were certain things I had to do, like get CORGI registered and get public liability insurance, and, of course, I had to get a van, because I was now going to be a worker out 'on the tools' – back to where I began. I got all that sorted, and I turned the study in the back of the house into an office and that was me. Ready to go, or so I thought.

I let all my contacts know I had left the business and would be setting up on my own.

For the first week or so, I was a bit lost because I was in relatively new territory, stuck in a wee office on my own in my house with nothing much happening. It was a different way of doing things! Gone was the hustle and bustle of the office with everyone coming and going at all times of the day. I just couldn't get used to being on my own. So, I bit the bullet and called Mary. I asked if she wanted to start part-time. I explained it was very early days and I had no work yet but was happy to pay her £60 a week on a part-time basis. I also said I would pay her more as the company grew and I could afford it. I was sure that together we could get it moving and generate enough business to make it a success. She agreed she would. I was happy and relieved she would be joining me. It would be just like old times!

I remember those early days with fondness. In the mornings, Mary would appear at the bottom of the street with her fur coat and the big hat she used to wear. I used to watch out for her so that I could put the kettle on because the first thing we would do every day was sit down for a chat and a cup of tea. Then we would get down to business.

The first thing we did was compose a letter to all the clients we had worked for at Maclean & Nuttall. This was an opportunity to appraise them of the new situation and that we were now in the market looking for work. So, we wrote to everybody we could think of, introducing Gas Call Services and asking for a meeting to discuss any opportunities that might be available and the various aspects of work that we could do, and how could we get on their approved contractors list, because that was how it used to work in those days. You had to be on that list before you got any work.

We got a limited response, which was not very encouraging, but I was offered several meetings with previous clients. While they were happy to see me and have a coffee and a chat and wish me well, they told me they could only use companies that had at least three years trading history. That was something I hadn't really thought about. It was clear this wasn't going to generate any work. I had to think of other ideas.

We put an advert in the *Yellow Pages*, and we wrote to anyone we could think of – Scottish Gas, insurance companies, facilities management companies and anyone who might give us a lead. We had leaflets printed up, and we used to take Vicki and Linzi to private housing estates on a Saturday where we would give them each a big bundle of leaflets to put through letterboxes. They got paid £5 each for that, and I think they enjoyed it. It was like a wee adventure. And we would usually go for a McDonald's when we were finished.

We were determined to make it work. We kept doing the leaflet drops and sending follow-up letters to the companies who had not responded to the first letter. We also kept pushing away at property management companies. We would get the odd job coming in, just here and there, but nothing of any substance. I was paying Mary, but I wasn't taking anything. I was just living on my savings. But I believed in us, and I knew we would get a break at some point. What I was paying Mary was only pin money. She always used to say that what I paid her wouldn't buy her a good lipstick! I used to wonder what the cost of a good lipstick was! I always told her

I would look after her and pay her much more when the company could afford it.

Eventually, we got some jobs from a property management company based in Govanhill. They employed contractors like us to do repairs. Most of the work was in and around Govanhill and predominantly for the Asian community. It was good to finally have some work, and especially in this area, because there were some perks! I remember the number of times I was working in Asian people's houses, and I would be asked if I was hungry. I would always say, 'Yes!' I knew they could turn out a really good, tasty meal, and it was much better than you could get in the restaurants. I was always keen to try anything anybody would give me, and it was always very good.

Slowly but surely, I built a good relationship with this property management company. They realised I was pretty reliable, and I was getting the jobs done without any comeback. The only thing was, they were slow at paying because they would wait until they got paid by the landlord before they would pay me so there was no risk for them. I usually got paid in the end, though.

Those were crazy days. I felt like Superman because I would be out in the morning wearing a suit and tie, banging on doors trying to meet potential clients, and in the afternoon, I would be out doing some jobs with my overalls on and up to my eyes in muck. I didn't know if I was coming or going in those days. Half the time, I would also have to run Mary home in the van. It was funny seeing Mary in her posh coat and hat getting into a van. It wasn't very becoming, but we just made do.

It was a struggle, but we persevered, and eventually, we began to get some work through the doors. And it was very satisfying when we were eventually awarded our first social housing contract, with Cube Housing Association, in late 1997. It was a good one to get because it covered various areas across Scotland and driving the van about would give us some publicity. Winning that contract was a validation of the hard work and commitment we had both shown, and I was proud of us. However, there was one problem. The representatives of Cube wanted to visit the offices and see our set-up. Obviously, it was only Mary and me, and we were still working out of the study in the house. That would never do! We needed to look professional, so I started looking for suitable premises that would present us in a better light.

I came across Westwood Business Centre in Easterhouse. It was an old school that had been converted into business units. There was loads of parking, there was a canteen, a dining area and a reception area with someone on the front desk. It seemed ideal for us, so I arranged a lease for the smallest unit available. This was a small room at the rear of the building on the second floor, but there was space for some desks and filing cabinets, so we were happy to snap it up. The entrance to the building was through a set of glass doors, and it was secured by key cards. There was always a receptionist on the desk and a security guy, so it all looked very professional. It also had all the facilities we needed, like fax machines and photocopiers and even a postal collection.

When the representatives from Cube arrived, I met them at reception and asked if they wanted to have a quick coffee. They were happy to sit in the canteen and have a chat. Luckily, they didn't want to visit the office. They were very impressed with the whole set-up, and they went away with the idea that we were as big as we had said we were, even though it was really just me and Mary.

This became our strategy, and it paid off. We used the exact same process for other potential customers and clients. No one knew how big or small an organisation we were since we always steered visitors towards the canteen for coffee. We quickly increased our client list, and soon we realised we had reached the stage where we would have to start employing people.

This in itself was scary. We didn't want people to think we were just a startup. We wanted to show employees there was plenty of work to be had and there was longevity in the work. Taking on employees meant we would have to have all the proper processes in place for things like deducting tax and National Insurance contributions. We also needed vehicles and tools and equipment. It all cost money, and it impacted the cashflow because I had put so much money in to start with. I was paying Mary, and I was paying rent on the business premises and I was still not taking in any money. At one point I had to borrow some money from my brother Francis, which was a good help. It was a case of pushing on as best I could. A lot had to happen before we were ready to bring people on board, but we did it.

And then it was all about picking the right people because up until then, I had been carrying out all the work, and they needed to meet my standards.

They were anxious times, trying to grow the business, but we kept our nerve. It was imperative we started to get things moving properly.

*Big Owen worked with me on building houses & then at Maclean & Nuttall &
ultimately Gas Call, he became a great friend.*

16. RHINDMUIR GROVE - PART 5: 1997 - 2001

Over the years, Mary and I had become close friends and confided in each other, and I knew she had some personal issues. One day in the summer of 1996 I was home when there was a knock at the door. I wasn't expecting anyone so I was surprised to see Mary and the girls. They all looked a bit bedraggled. Apparently, they had been on a day out near Loch Lomond and had gone into a rain-soaked field where there had been some cows and they had got covered in mud. They had been on the way home but had decided to pop in and see me as it was on the way. I insisted that the girls, Vicki and Linzi should freshen up, and whilst they were doing that Mary and I had a cup of tea and a chat. That chat would have a big impact on all our lives as we decided that Mary and the girls would come and stay at Rhindmuir Grove to see how that would work out. It might work, it might not but we thought we would give it a try.

After all, I had a big house with plenty of room, so it seemed to make sense, although it was a big commitment for both of us. Uprooting Linzi and Vicki and moving them into a new house would be a challenge, even though they knew me well. And how would Kara and Mikaela react? It was their house too. There was a lot to consider.

Whatever I felt for Mary, our relationship at that time was platonic, of course. She and the girls slept in separate rooms. We were great friends, and Mary knew she would be safe with me.

Although we had known each other for about 6 years, it took a lot of adjustment before things started running smoothly. Trying to get used to living together under the same roof was a bit different from working together! There were quite a few times their bags were packed and unpacked again! There were some challenging times, to say the least, for everybody. All the girls reacted differently, and although we tried everything we could think of, in the end, it took a few years to settle down. Every summer, we took the girls on holiday to Magaluf. It was great fun but always a bit of a challenge. Kara and Mikaela were being taken out of their comfort zone, and they were still young. Mary did her best to accommodate Kara and Mikaela. It took some work, and there were anxious times, but eventually, we had great holidays together and created some good memories.

Despite all the challenges, it was quite a special time for me. Ann and I had divorced in 1998, so I was a free man. I loved having Mary around. In fact, I was falling in love with her. I don't know if she realised at the time, but as far as I was concerned, it was true love. I even told my mum if I was ever to remarry, it would be to Mary. She was the perfect woman for me.

While our personal lives were changing for the better, Gas Call had become quite successful in picking up contracts in and around the Easterhouse area. It was a big day when we started our first employee. And soon after that, Big Garth joined us. He had worked for me at Maclean & Nuttall, and we knew we could trust him. We actually left him in charge when we went on our first holiday abroad together. That was a bit scary, leaving a gas fitter in charge of our fledgling business! But it all passed off without any issue.

As we grew the business, we had to employ office staff as well as gas fitters, and some of them are still with us to this day. And I didn't forget my old friends, either. Terry Maclean's new business, Gas Care Scotland, was carrying out gas safety audits, which were a new process within the industry. It wasn't doing so well because people hadn't switched on to it, and Terry was struggling to make it work. I passed as much work as I could to Terry to help him out. In November 1999, I eventually bought him out of Gas Care Scotland. I then gave him a full-time job with all the benefits. He had been travelling up and down to Glasgow from Dingwall, and it was costing him a fortune in fuel. Now he had a car, a fuel card and a guaranteed salary and that made his life a lot easier. He embraced his new role and got heavily involved in what we were doing. It was great to have the team back together!

The business just kept growing. It was a big moment when we had a cash balance of £100,000 in the bank!

We had to take on extra office space to accommodate our growing staff, and we also took on a stores-cum-depot at Blairtummock industrial estate so that the engineers and the supervisors could operate efficiently. We had come a long way in a short time, and we were doing well. We had grown turnover from £47,000 in the first year to £1.7 million, and it was only 1999. I was proud of what we had achieved in such a short time.

We were getting to the stage where we had critical mass. Gone were the days when I would have to leave the house on Christmas Day and travel to breakdowns and so on just to keep the money coming in. Now that we had all the engineers, I didn't have to be out 'on the tools' so much. I could focus on growing the company.

As Gas Call grew, we started to attract some media attention. At first, I resisted, but eventually, I succumbed. It was so strange seeing my story in the newspapers! I had come a long way from the tenement block in Springburn.

In 2002, my accountant told me about a competition called Inner City 100. The idea was to recognise and celebrate 100 companies that had demonstrated exponential growth despite being based in the inner cities. Easterhouse, where we were based, fitted the bill. I agreed we would submit an application. What did we have to lose?

For the competition, we had to do a presentation in front of some high-powered businesspeople, including Anita Roddick, the founder and owner of the Body Shop. I was pretty nervous, but when the time came, it all went well. There was a drinks reception afterwards, and Anita Roddick pushed her way through the crowd to me. She wanted to meet the plumber who had grown his business by over 2000%. She was very bubbly and enthusiastic. But I had to point out I was a gas fitter, not a plumber! I'm not sure she understood the difference!

We were told we had won, which was a fantastic result since it was the first time we had entered a competition. But before it had properly sunk in, they told us we hadn't won. This was because one of the requirements was to have a full three years' worth of accounts, which we didn't because we had changed the accounting period in the first year. So, we were placed second, which was still quite an achievement. We would have to go to London for the awards ceremony, so that was something to look forward to. Then I got a letter inviting me to Downing Street for a drinks reception to meet Gordon Brown. It was all very exciting!

Before the awards ceremony, a film company came to Glasgow to make a documentary-type film – starring me! I was finally able to put my movie experience to good use! It was basically telling my story against a background of the dereliction and broken-down buildings in Easterhouse, and it would be screened at the awards ceremony. It was gloomy, but it was my second time in front of the cameras, and I just lapped it up!

Mary and I flew down to London for the ceremony. For security reasons, I had to attend Downing Street by myself. The taxi driver who took me there thought I was joking at first, and I had to persuade him it was true! I was really going to Downing Street to meet the chancellor of the exchequer, who would later become prime minister. On the way there, I told the taxi driver my story, and by the time we arrived, he was insisting he would get his grandson into gas fitting because clearly it was a good business to get into!

Notwithstanding all this excitement and recognition of our success, Mary and I had been working hard and growing the business. We were still living together, and we had become a real partnership, spending all of our time together, so it was only natural that we both fell in love. I had known for some time she was the one for me, but it was wonderful to find out she felt the same. Although our first marriages had ended in divorce, we were open to trying again. We talked about it a few times, but nothing too serious. We were together now, and nothing would change that.

One evening in early summer, we were at a little restaurant called Number 16 in the West End of Glasgow. We were chatting about what the budget would be if we got married, and we agreed it would be between £5,000 and £10,000, which was a significant sum back then. We were distracted, however, when our food arrived. I had never had a lamb shank before, but for some reason, I had ordered one that evening. Up walked the waitress carrying this big leg of lamb with bones sticking out! I was flabbergasted. My face must have been a picture. Mary was hysterical with laughter. She knew I wouldn't be able to eat it. She had learned a lot from the days of the prawn sandwich! Kind as ever, she offered me her dish, which I quickly accepted. Neither of us went hungry!

On the way home, we were driving up Montrose Street, which had a very steep hill. Halfway up the hill, I suddenly pulled the car over and got out. Mary had no idea what was going on, and I wasn't 100% sure myself. I went round to Mary's side and opened her door. She looked at me as if I had gone mad, and perhaps for a moment I had. There, in the middle of a Glasgow Street in the early evening, I got down on one knee and asked her to marry me.

She looked into my eyes and said yes!

We set about making arrangements right away as there was no point in waiting. We looked at several venues and ended up with the Bothwell Bridge Hotel in Bothwell, which we booked for 2nd December 2000. It wasn't going to be a white wedding because we had both been married before, but the weather might make it so! December was a strange time to get married. It was a bit frantic, but we made all the arrangements in time because we knew we wanted to do it. Kara, Mikaela, Vicki and Linzi would be bridesmaids, and my pal Terry Maclean would be my best man. We would be in kilts, which was strange because I had never worn a kilt before!

We had to organise a vicar and post banns and all that, so as expected, we went over the budget! We ended up having a great day. It was a huge success, and it was really nice to see all the friends and family together, especially my brothers dressed up in kilts, which made my mum very proud. It was a very fast-moving and emotional day. Mary was a beautiful bride, and her dress was stunning. I will always remember how it felt when I turned around and saw her walking up the aisle towards me. It was a feeling like no other.

All the daughters were beautiful as well. Now we were truly a family. It was a spectacular day for the start of our married life together, and I was a very proud and happy man.

December is a very busy month for us with family birthdays and Christmas festivities, so we only booked a few days in the

Dornoch Castle Hotel for our honeymoon. This is a beautiful place in the north of Scotland near the coast, and we were looking forward to a few days of quiet peace together. However, fate had other ideas.

Unbeknownst to us, Madonna and her soon-to-be husband, Guy Ritchie, were getting their son, Rocco, christened at Dornoch Cathedral the day before their wedding at Skibo Castle. The place was awash with media, and it was crazy. We thought we were going to a quiet village! We were watching it all with amazement when someone in the crowd told the media we were on honeymoon. Of course, they were keen for any kind of comparison with the famous pair, and before we knew it, we were live on breakfast TV being interviewed by Richard Bacon! It was really funny because a lot of our pals were expecting to see Madonna on TV, and they saw us instead!

It was a few moments of fame just when we weren't expecting it!

Me outside 10 Downing Street after meeting Gordon Brown.

Me and Mary my beautiful wife on our wedding day.

17. RHINDMUIR GROVE - PART 6: 2001 - 2004

Although the honeymoon was a bit more exciting than we had anticipated, we still had a lovely time and it was over all too quickly. Then it was back home to get the festive season and birthdays over and done with and to welcome in the year 2001. A year that would see another big change for Gas Call Services, and Ken Maclean's return to the industry.

In the last year or so, we had probably expanded a bit faster than we should have. We were doing work across Scotland, and we had also picked up work with Scottish Power. There had recently been a deregulation of the supply industries for electricity and gas, and Scottish Power had started to supply gas as well as electricity. We had picked up the contract to do safety checks for them, and it was mental. They didn't just supply Scotland, so we were sending engineers into England, particularly Manchester, and as far south as Brighton. It was quite a challenge.

After his wife's death, Ken Maclean had spent some time with family and concentrated on his music. Now a few years had passed, and in late 2001, he was ready to get back into the business. He approached me with a proposition. Shaun, his nephew, owned a company called Apollo Heating. Ken's plan was to create a group of companies with Gas Call and

Apollo Heating. I was a bit reluctant as Apollo had just been incorporated in June that year, and I wasn't sure how viable it was. I felt Apollo Heating didn't have the same standards as we had, but Ken had come in and got involved, and he knew how to run businesses, so no doubt it would be a success.

I talked it over with Mary, and we decided to consider the deal. Ken had previous experience of working across the UK, and because of the challenges we were facing, as far as I was concerned it would be far better to have Ken on board to help us manage it.

Firstly, we went through the process of valuing Gas Call. In that year, our accounts had taken a bit of a dip, so I was on the back foot a wee bit. I wasn't confident of the real value of the business, and I didn't really agree with it because I knew all the ins and outs of it. However, we did our due diligence, and after several meetings up and down the country, Ken and I decided we were going to do something together.

We considered exchanging shares in the companies instead of cash, and I was a bit reluctant. The fact was, I wanted cash because that was what drove me on. I continued talks with Ken.

On 11th September, we were in a meeting in my office in Westwood. It was just a normal day, and we expected nothing more than continuing our discussions and maybe socialising afterwards. Suddenly, Mary burst through the door. She told us that a plane had flown into one of the Twin Towers in New York City. We thought it must be some sort of mistake. We pulled up the news on the computer and watched as the second plane hit the second tower. It was horrific. Was it a terrorist attack? Were we watching the start of the Third World War?

It really did seem like that. We were glued to the screen as the drama unfolded. Then the news came in about the Pentagon getting hit as well. We couldn't believe what we were seeing. We watched the collapse of the towers in disbelief. It just didn't seem real. Here we were, sitting talking about business and money and all the rest of it, and then this was playing out in front of us. Work didn't seem all that important anymore.

Nearly 3,000 people died in that terrorist attack. What had humanity come to? It was a day that will stay etched in my memory forever.

But life – and business – goes on. I eventually agreed terms with Ken, and I travelled down to his solicitor's office in Manchester to finalise the deal. I didn't have legal representation with me, which was naive of me when I look back on it. However, we went through all the paperwork and signed it accordingly, and I walked out of that office still a shareholder in Gas Call and also part of a bigger group. I wasn't a major shareholder, but at the end of the day, it is better to have a chunk of something than a chunk of nothing; that's how I look at it. I had a deal that would see me turn over some serious money over the next three years. If I had been braver and less naive, I would probably have done a better deal than the one I did, but it was a lesson that was learned for the future.

I'd set the business up in 1996, and I hardly did any work in that first year. Within five years of trading, I was part of a bigger group of companies that covered the UK. It was a good feeling. I also had a big fat cheque in my hand and some serious money to follow in an earnout. It was surreal. I was a boy from Springburn who had left school without any qualifications; now, I was holding this cheque that I had earned through my own hard work and perseverance. I had really achieved something.

Now I was in a comfortable place with Gas Call, I had a little bit of time to spend on my other interests. One of these was patents, and I had engaged in a few ideas via Murgitroyd's in Glasgow. One particular item we set up was an 'access unit', which was something that helped with a specific problem experienced by landlords.

To meet their legislative requirements, gas appliances in rented accommodation had to be serviced every year. The problem was that some tenants, particularly social housing tenants, wouldn't let gas engineers into the property. In those days, it was a 50% failure rate. So, we came up with this idea of an access unit. This was a device that could be set to turn the heating off, so the tenant would have to call up the landlord and say, 'My heating's not working.' Then the engineer would get in and carry out the service visit at that point, and the landlord would meet his legislative requirements.

I set up a company called Intelihome to promote the access unit, and we had actually filed this for patent and had cracked on with manufacturing before we found out another company had put in a patent only a couple of months before us. We weren't very happy, and we decided to challenge this patent in the High Court in London before Lord Justice Laddie. Unfortunately, we actually lost the case and had to pay damages. After that, we spent a lot of time, money and effort trying to re-engineer the units, but the wind was knocked out of our sails and we decided to give up on it.

However, we had more success with another invention, which dated back to when I was working with Maclean & Nuttall on the Glasgow City Council contract. We were usually doing about 1,000 heating installations a year for GCC. And one of the snagging issues that kept cropping up was the fitting of the pressure relief outlets at high level. This was a device that would safely exit hot water to the outside if the system pressure increased.

What tended to happen was that the guys doing the installation would usually leave it to the end of the day. They would pop a pipe out, intending to go back and finish it, but it might be dark or raining or they might forget about it. That meant they would leave a pipe sticking out of the wall, and if the pressure relief valve did come into play, then it meant that hot water could be expelled out of the open pipe and could land on a person or a dog, so there was a danger. When the guys didn't complete this work, we would have to get someone else to go round and do it because otherwise the clerk of works wouldn't sign it off and we wouldn't get paid.

I had an idea to solve this in my head for years, and finally I got round to doing some drawings and a description, and I submitted an application for a patent. I branded my device the Pro Term, which was an acronym for Pressure Relief

Outlet Termination. Eventually, I got the patent for it, and we were ready to go.

At that time, copper prices were escalating to an extent that would make the production process prohibitive, so I made a plastic version using suitable heat-resistant products. This allowed for the successful creation of the end product. There were challenges, however. To make it a success, we had to change industry perceptions, and that took about five years. A lot of time was lost for production and marketing, and I didn't want to waste time and money pursuing this when there was no guarantee of the outcome. I put it on the back burner. My time was needed elsewhere, and there was resistance to the product. And I had to get the British Safety Council to change the standard, and that doesn't happen overnight!

But I did eventually get the standard changed, which was a great achievement, and I could move forward with the product and people would accept it.

I kept coming up with ideas for patents, and while there was mileage in some of them, there were always challenges. I had an idea for a digital road crossing sign with a rechargeable battery so people would clearly see it in the dark and when there was poor visibility. I came up with triangular cabling for overhead cables so that water wouldn't freeze on them and bring them down. Another idea was a boiler in a box for fitting and replacing boilers where all the pipe work would be concealed, and it would be more aesthetically pleasing. I also had an idea for a headrest for coach travel in aeroplanes, which has been granted, though I've not had the time to commercialise it.

I still have lots of ideas, but the challenge is the time and effort needed to bring them to fruition, and focusing on these particular items isn't one of my priorities.

18. RHINDMUIR GROVE - PART 7: 2004

As the years passed, bringing me success in business and happiness in my personal life, the people around me were changing, getting older, and in some cases, wiser. We were always a close family, and whilst I loved all my brothers and sisters dearly, I always felt closest to my mum. She was a colossus in our lives.

She was born Elizabeth Finlay in Springburn in 1927, but she was known as Betty. She was first child of my Granny Jessie and Granda Arthur Finlay and the eldest of eight kids, five girls and three boys. That was a tough period to be brought up in. As a child, she watched her younger sister Jessie die of consumption, and then a second sister, also Jessie, die at 18. This must have been heartbreaking for her and the whole family. It was a terrible, terrible time in the history of our country, and I don't think it was that uncommon for people to die very young. She was closest to her sister Vera, and they continued to be best pals throughout their lives. So close, in fact, that Betty and Vera had a double wedding in 1953 when they had both married husbands called Frank – Frank Donnelly and Frank Sheldon. Before that, my mum worked as a clippie on the buses. When we all came along, of course, she had to spend all her time bringing us up. With a family of seven children, there would have been hard times through the years, but they both did an upstanding job.

Even with the demands of her family, my mum always had an active social life. She was quite popular, and she and my dad seemed to get on with anybody. She also loved bingo, not just to win but for the social side. She and Dad used to meet up with Vera, Uncle Frank and their daughter at the bingo, and even my old granda used to go. And that was just the start. Most of the time, other family members would also turn up. It could be quite an outing, with maybe 10 or 12 Donnellys and Finlays all going to the bingo together. When she went to bingo, all we kids would wait up to see what she brought back. In the early days when she won, she would bring back a fish supper to share out. If not, it would be a single Mars bar we had to cut up so each one got a piece. When I was a bit older, I would sometimes go along myself, just to see everyone.

As we grew up, we stayed a close family. Over the years, only my brother Francis and I lived away. Everyone else stayed in Glasgow, and after my dad died, I moved back to spend more time with my mum.

She had spent her life bringing up seven children, and she had been looking forward to spending her retirement with my dad. This dream was taken away from her when he died, and she spent the next 14 years just wanting to be with him.

She would always talk about Frank and how she missed him, but she was a very strong woman. Because of the type of job I did, I could actually get away when she needed me. So, whenever there was a funeral or anything, I would volunteer to take my mum. My mum was the oldest, and all her younger brothers and sisters died before her, except for Vera, who outlived her and only died recently. It was a shame watching her attend these funerals for all her brothers and sisters. I used to sit there in the chapel and wonder what she must be thinking because that's just not the way it's supposed to be. But that's what happens in life. I loved my mum, and I used to tell her as often as I could because I had never told my dad, and I didn't want to make the same mistake twice.

My mum had COPD, but she still smoked like a 'lum', and she loved her cigarettes and coffee. She would get annoyed when I wouldn't bring any duty free fags back from Spain or wherever I had been. It was against my principles to help her smoke. I was totally anti-smoking since it had nearly killed me after an operation when I was in my teens.

I had been at a stag night with a group of work colleagues. We were just having a good time when I looked around and saw a guy getting bullied. Even though they were work colleagues I didn't really know either of the people involved, I just couldn't stand by and let it happen. I stepped in between them, and suddenly, the bully headbutted me. Pain exploded in my head, and for a moment, I didn't know where I was. Blood poured from my nose and went all down my good clothes. I cleaned myself up and waved it off. Probably I was anaesthetised from all the beer.

The next morning, my nose was swollen right up, and I couldn't breathe properly. I got some nasal inhalers to try to ease it, but days later, it still wasn't getting any better and I was feeling a bit unwell. Eventually, I went to the hospital. It was calm in the waiting room, but when I eventually got seen by a doctor, it all started to happen really fast. It turned out my septum was badly broken, and I had sepsis that was spreading through my bloodstream. They had to do an emergency operation to save my life.

Apparently, I was lucky to survive. After the operation, I was advised to stop smoking, and I gave up completely. I have been against smoking ever since. But Mum was unconvinced, and she never gave up.

She was a great pal to everybody, and we all loved her very much. In 2004, she started getting poorly and was in and out of hospital for a while. When they could do no more for her, she ended up in the Marie Curie Hospice. We knew she wouldn't be there for long, so we visited whenever we could. She was hardly ever left to sit by herself. One time, when Mary and I visited, she told us that she had been out for a lovely walk round the garden and all that, which we thought was a bit odd. It turned out one of the nurses had told her to close her eyes and to imagine the walk. I'm not sure if she actually knew it was in her imagination. It was one of the things that indicated she was getting near the end. It was a sad time.

She hated being in the hospice, and she wanted to go home. I wanted to look after her, so we considered if we could have her at Rhindmuir Grove. The study was downstairs and near a toilet, and we looked into putting a bed in there. It was probably too late by then. Mum did get out of the hospice briefly, but before we knew it, she was back in hospital and she quickly became very poorly.

The night came when she was dropping in and out of consciousness, murmuring about Frank and her mum and dad. I stayed with her the whole night, gently wetting her lips with a cotton swab to ensure that she was getting some liquids. I thought the end had come, and I told her several times throughout the night that it was OK to go. But she was having none of that. She was hanging on. She was a fighter.

In the morning, I called round my brothers and sisters and said, 'You should come to the hospital. I don't think Mum will last much longer.'

Everybody duly arrived, and we all sat around her bed, speaking about the good old days and holding her hand. She was unconscious, but I was sure she knew we were there. It was a long, hard day, but eventually, like all things, it passed. As the day ended, her skin changed from pale to grey, and I could see the life draining out of her. I told everyone her time had come.

Jim shouted, 'No! Not yet!' But it made no difference.

It was a very humbling and privileged experience to be there at the end. I remember taking a picture of Mum with everyone around her. And when it was developed there was a strange glow around her, almost as if her soul was leaving her body at that very minute. It was 10 past 10 on 12th November 2004. Her long life was over, and she would finally be with Dad again. That's what she had wanted for the past 14 years. She was 77 years old when she died.

The funeral was well attended. Ashleigh, my niece, spoke some words at the service, and so did I. They were words just for my mum, which I had written down and placed in her coffin. I wish now I had kept a copy.

It was a very sad day, but to know that Mum and Dad were together again gave us all great comfort.

Me with my Auntie Vera 14th March 2017.

My Mum and Dad's double wedding day with Uncle Frank and Auntie Vera with my Gran and Granda Finlay in the background.

19. RHINDMUIR GROVE - PART 8: 2004 - 2007

2004 was a very sad and difficult year, and we were glad when it was over.

As the year turned, Mary and I needed something to help us recover and move on with our lives. We needed to get away for a while, and instead of our usual holiday abroad, we decided to try something different. 2005 became the year we discovered cruising.

Our first trip was on the *Oceana,* owned by P&O Cruises. It was all new to us, and we wondered what the dress code on board would be. This was especially important to Mary, who needed to know what she should pack. We asked a pal who used to go cruising, Tom Maitland, if we needed to take anything formal. He said, 'You don't need to bother about that.'

Reassured, Mary just took some summer dresses. And, of course, when we went down to dinner the first night, it was all evening wear. The clothes we had brought just weren't suitable. We had to get something new, and quickly.

The first place we docked was Barcelona. Instead of going around looking at all the wonderful sights, we spent the day rushing around trying to find suitable attire for the trip. Going into shops where the assistants only spoke Spanish was a big challenge! Luckily, it worked out, and we could relax for the rest of the trip.

Although Mary wasn't sure about cruising at first, by the end of the trip, she was crying because she didn't want to get off the boat! We were hooked on cruises from then on, and we have been on several every year since. We always get suites, which is very expensive but worth every penny. One year, we had the penthouse suite, which was fantastic. There is truly nothing like it.

However, while we were away on our first cruise, one of the guys who worked for us, Dennis Crammond, left Gas Call and set up a business with Kenny Henderson, who had previously worked for us. They called it City Technical Services. They started to poach our contracts and manpower, and slowly but surely, the work we got in Glasgow diminished. This really annoyed me because we were a Glasgow-based company and had been recognised as such by the Inner City 100. Ultimately, I couldn't get work in Glasgow for love nor money. Luckily, we had other contracts that kept the business growing.

And because it was growing, I could help support my family. My mum, when she was alive, asked if I could do anything for my brothers, so I did. I put my brother Jim through his driving test and his apprenticeship and brought him into the business, where he still works to this day. I also gave my brother Brian a job. He was a driver and labourer. He worked for me on and off for years, and despite our best efforts to make it work we ended up parting ways. That was a bit disappointing at the time but not everything works out and Brian went on to find success as a self-employed taxi driver.

During their University years, both Vicki and Linzi had part-time jobs within Gas Call before they embarked on their long-term careers. For Vicki, working on reception would lead to something very special for her and ultimately have a big impact on Gas Call.

A guy called Alan Lowe came to us as an engineer from Scottish Gas, and he soon took a shine to Vicki. He found out she loved strawberry tarts, so he used to bring them in for her to try to woo her. It wasn't long before he was successful!

They married in 2007 at St. Bridget's church in Baillieston, and the reception was held at the Bothwell Bridge Hotel, the same place Mary and I held our reception.

The wedding went off without a hitch. It was a great day, and everybody had a wonderful time. However, there was one part of the day that gave me some real anxiety. It was the speeches. Vicki was the first daughter to get married, and I had to step up. It was the first time I had done such a thing. It was murder.

I was so nervous when I stood up to speak that I was swaying from side to side. I got a lot of heckling and lots of funny comments at my expense, but I got through it in the end, though I don't know how! At that point, I decided I was never, ever going to do another speech without some help.

Despite that, it was a great day and night that passed in a flash. Before we knew it, the bride and groom were leaving to go to their hotel in the city, where they were staying before they went to the Maldives on their honeymoon the next day.

Everybody was cheering, and we bid them all farewell and wished them good luck. We didn't expect to hear from them again until after the honeymoon, and we went back to the party. It wasn't long before we got a call from Alan and Vicki. Vicki was in tears. The hotel they had booked had double-booked their room and everywhere was full.

They were devastated. Of course, Saturday night, trying to find a hotel was almost impossible, especially that Saturday as there was a big Scotland rugby international game on. Vicki was in tears, makeup ruined, and all the rest of it. Eventually, Alan got them into the Devonshire Gardens, which is a prestigious hotel. They didn't know how much it would cost, but Alan was so relieved to get there he just turned his sporran out and said, 'Give me a room – that will cover it!'

What a relief! It was very stressful at the time, though we all laugh about it now.

With Ken on board, the business continued to grow and be successful. We won the ACHA contract to install heating systems and rewire houses across Argyll and Bute. It was a rural area, but we had already operated the service and maintenance contract, so we had some experience of operating there and that would become something we would continue to hold for 10 years.

Winning this contract was a major shift in our footprint across Scotland, and naturally, this drew some attention. We started getting quite a lot of interest from potential suitors, including some well-known PLCs. It was very gratifying after all our hard work.

One day, I got a call from a guy called Carl Chambers. He represented a company called Spice PLC. They were looking to expand their footprint into Scotland, and Carl wanted to discuss a possible acquisition of Gas Call Services. This was the big time! Arrangements were made for Ken and me to meet Carl and discuss the potential for a merger. At the meeting, we also mentioned there was a sister company, Apollo Heating. Carl expressed an interest in Apollo as well.

It was agreed that due diligence would be carried out on Gas Call Services. Unfortunately, it was just at the time Gas Call's numbers had taken a wee bit of a tumble. This was due to a particular contract with Scottish Gas. It was a kind of ad hoc agreement where we would do only what they needed us to do at any given time, so the numbers could fluctuate up and down. It was a bit low at that point, and our numbers were affected. The timing was terrible. Despite our best efforts to persuade Spice PLC this was normal for the industry, they decided to put any position on hold and see how things fared.

However, the same could not be said for Apollo Heating, and within a few months, they agreed a deal worth in excess of £10 million. And I missed out on that because I had rejected the option of a share exchange between Apollo and Gas Call!

These things happen, but it was a bit of a blow. My focus was now to recover revenue and show Spice that Gas Call was worth just as much. It was all about timing. I remember taking representatives from Spice on the long journey to Oban to get confirmation that the ACHA contract would, in fact, deliver the anticipated revenues. We drove through some remote locations, and we came across several Gas Call Services vehicles out there. That had a bit of an impact, and they were impressed. We also saw a lift in the revenue from Scottish Gas as they started to increase our work levels. In due course, it all came together, and in 2007, Spice PLC finally acquired Gas Call Services in a multi-million-pound deal. Timing was everything!

The deal was done in a hotel near Leeds, and there was a lot of to-ing and fro-ing right up to the last minute, but we signed the paperwork just before midnight on the day of the deadline. It was surreal – the deal made us all very wealthy, and it had happened just as I hoped it would. My aspiration was to become a millionaire by the time I was 50. The deal was done in early December, mere weeks before my 50th birthday at the end of the month. I had made it!

All the champagne corks were popping, and everybody was congratulating themselves on a job well done. It was the culmination of a lot of hard work and an endorsement of our efforts to achieve success.

Job done.

Vicki and Alan on their wedding day.

20. RHINDMUIR GROVE - PART 9:
2007 - 2009

After the acquisition of Gas Call Services by Spice, the PLC culture began to set in, just like it had after the acquisition of Maclean & Nuttall by Schlumberger, which had driven both Mary and me out of the company. Would the same thing happen again? Would history repeat itself?

It did. There was tension in the air, and the staff were divided. Some were loyal to us, but others were not. There were clashes in every area, and I began to wonder who to trust. My email account was even hacked! I was livid about that, and ultimately, I had to sack the people involved. It was obvious that the corporate PLC culture and the private business culture were very far apart. Mary and I could see that what they were doing was destined for failure. The writing was on the wall.

So, we got ready for the inevitable next step. We rebranded Intelihome as Intelihome (UK) Ltd and set it up to take on gas work.

Mary left first. She went to work for Intelihome and took two of the staff, Lyndsey and Evonne, with her. I knew I would be barred from poaching any staff if I left, so I poached them before instead.

Around 18 months after acquiring Gas Call, Spice made a bid for City Technical Services. This had grown to be one of our major competitors and had been acquired by E.ON, even though it was still run by my two disloyal ex-employees. The idea was to relocate City Technical's business into the building next to us and run the whole operation from one location. I had reservations about the proposal, and given all the additional workload that I would have, I realised I wouldn't have any time to enjoy the money I had made from the sale of Gas Call. I advised Spice PLC they would need more money from E.ON to take on City Technical, and also, they would need someone to run the new business as I would be leaving.

Spice took my advice, and instead of requesting more money, they pulled out of the deal. They lost favour with E.ON, and it caused a bit of an upset. I went on garden leave, and Mary and I set off on a Mediterranean cruise. While I was on the cruise, I received an email telling me not to return to the office. They instructed a manager to have the locks changed and to pack up my stuff for collection. It made my blood boil.

It was clear that Spice was in trouble. Their gas business model clearly wasn't working. Just to rub salt into the wound, we set up new offices for Intelihome directly below Gas Call Services, refurbished to a high standard with all the latest equipment. When anyone from Spice visited, they had to pass our offices first. We made sure there was a big sign just so they understood there was still competition out there. Mary, Lyndsey, Evonne and I all worked hard to get new contracts as best we could. We didn't have much work at first – we were back to square one yet again. But I was confident I could build up Intelihome to a significant level.

I had a plan.

I persuaded Alan that Gas Call Services should subcontract some work to Intelihome. This worked for a while, and Intelihome also secured contracts with Scottish Gas and City Building for service and maintenance. It wasn't long before our revenues started to go up, and our manpower was starting to pick up, too. Gas Call Services noticed this and started to mess us about with workloads and payment. Ultimately, we fell out with them completely.

However, we stuck to our guns. We concentrated on service and maintenance work and quickly grew the business to £1 million plus turnover in the first year.

Spice rebranded their gas business as Liberty Gas, and I monitored it closely, as I did with all competition. It wasn't long before Spice carried out a strategic review. Liberty Gas was losing millions, and they decided to dispose of it. History was repeating itself yet again.

I saw an opportunity to get Gas Call Services back at that point, but the bid was rejected because Spice wanted to get rid of the whole business, not just carve it up. Ultimately, Shaun Maclean acquired the whole of Liberty Gas.

Shaun told me he didn't want to operate in Scotland, and I saw my chance. We entered negotiations for Mary and me to reacquire Gas Call Services. It was quite a quick turnaround. The negotiations were tough, but I knew they wanted to offload Gas Call and I would win out in the end. I was successful, of course, and we ended up reacquiring Gas Call Services for the princely sum of £1.

I thought that was a fair price for both parties. But you know, it's a crazy number. We had sold the business in a multi-million-pound deal, and now we were getting it back for £1.

We used one of our other companies, Mima Enterprises UK Limited, as a holding company. Mima was a shell company I had formed in 2003, using the first two letters of my name and Mary's. It had been a dormant company, but now it was just what we needed as a vehicle to help create a group of companies. Mima Enterprises (UK) Ltd became the holding company, and it now owned Gas Call Services Ltd and Gas Care Scotland Ltd.

We were still operating Intelihome (UK) Ltd, which we held outside the group, just because we thought that was the best thing to do. Life was about to become very busy because we had to make things happen yet again. I loaned Mima £100,000 as working capital to keep Gas Call Services operational. The business was in serious decline. Turnover in 2009 was circa £6 million, and this had reduced to £2.1 million. A dramatic drop in turnover in one year. And it was making heavy losses. There was clearly a lot to do, and I would have to look at how to mitigate these losses. But first, we had to see how things stood.

It was a strange day when we walked back into the Gas Call Services office. It was interesting to see the reaction from the staff. Some were happy to see us, and some were not. There were a lot of people Mary and I had looked after and shown loyalty to, and in our absence, they had been disloyal to us. People were embarrassed, and some were afraid.

There were a lot of rumours flying about, including rumours of job losses. Some people just jumped before they were pushed. But our intention was to make the business work, not to take revenge. Certainly, people who had shown a complete lack of loyalty would be asked to leave, but others would stay with us. Alan decided to stay on at Liberty Gas as he was enjoying his experience there at that time.

A complete rebuild of the management team was required. Mary, Evonne, Lyndsey and I still had Intelihome to run, so we would have dual roles. Effectively, we were running two businesses side by side from the same building. They were different legal entities, and given the change in ownership, there was a lot of negotiation to be done with different suppliers. And we had to deal with the bank, which was a challenge and required additional securities to be put in place.

Mary and I took it all in our stride. It was a case of onwards and upwards.

21. BOTHWELL ROAD - PART 1:
2009 - 2010

The Bothwell Bridge Hotel has played quite a big part in our lives. Over the years, we held various family functions there, and Mary and I used to go there for lunch quite often. We had a real fondness for the place and the local area. After our lunches, we would sometimes drive around admiring all the beautiful sandstone buildings. We used to wonder how people could afford them and if they would ever come up for sale. Much as we liked Rhindmuir Grove, it was still the house I had built, and we had never had a house we had chosen together. At that time, Mary wanted to extend Rhindmuir Grove to create a larger family room to the rear and was having trouble persuading me to do it because I didn't really like the idea.

On one such day, in early 2009, we were driving around as usual, and we saw a 'For Sale' sign outside one of the beautiful houses on Bothwell Road. We looked at each other with excitement. This house could be just what we were looking for. It was an area we could see ourselves living in.

The owner had been a sheriff, no less, and he and his family had lived in it for the past 40 years. Now the family had flown the nest, and he had passed away, so it was only the mother, a retired schoolteacher, who was rattling around the house on her own. She had decided to downsize, and so it was on the market.

We arranged a viewing, and we fell in love with the house the moment we stepped in the door. It was beautiful. It was full of wonderful Victorian features like stained glass windows, ceiling roses and coving. There was even an old stable that still had the stable doors and all the old features. We loved it all. Now, all we had to do was get it. We put in several offers before finally having our last offer accepted. Coincidentally, I took the call on the same cruise that we were on when Spice PLC sacked me!

I was effectively unemployed, and now we had this new house, which would become a money pit. Although it was fabulous in its bones, it was in a poor state. The ceilings had been lowered, and it was stuck in the '70s, with an outdated kitchen and extensive use of Fyfestone. It would need a complete refurbishment.

But we never back down from a challenge! We wanted in before Christmas, so work started in earnest. The task was enormous. We had to sandblast and clean the outside. We had to sand all the internal floors, though ultimately, we had to replace them. We had to put in new wiring and plumbing, knock down walls, fix gutters . . . everything you could imagine that needed to be done to bring an old house into the modern age.

The previous owner had used the stable as a garage, but we had large and prestigious cars, and we felt that such a tight space wasn't going to work for us. We decided to put in a drive at the side of the building. Because it was a conservation area, we had issues with the council and the neighbours, but ultimately, it all worked out. It was just another challenge, and by then, we were used to overcoming whatever life threw at us!

We weren't scared of anything, and we just cracked on with the rebuild. Now we were running the two companies in tandem and trying to settle into a new house while still trying to sell Rhindmuir Grove. Lucky number two! The fact that we still had the old house turned out to be a blessing, because even though we had moved into the new house, there were still some issues with plumbing, and so we were able to go back to Rhindmuir Grove and use the showers and so on. That became the norm for a while.

We had settled back into Gas Call Services relatively well. The staff seemed happy that we were back after the overall poor management from the previous team. Morale had been low, but now they were optimistic that we would stabilise the business and get it back into profit. And this, in turn, would secure their jobs.

We quickly secured new contracts, one of which was from EAGA to deliver a contract for the Scottish government to install high efficiency boilers to heat homes and to make them more energy efficient. This was good solid work and would help to build revenue and profit. EAGA emailed to suggest I should use the Flowflex pipe cowl in any installation process. I opened the email attachment. It showed a shiny copper fitting that returned expelled water safely to the wall from overheated heating systems. Immediately, we realised this did the same as my Pro Term and that it infringed my patent rights. I forwarded the email on to my patent attorney expressing my concern. They advised me to contact Flowflex and explain.

I made a call to Flowflex and spoke to Peter Cull, who was the company secretary and financial director. I explained that I thought their pipe cowl was infringing my patent. They were a big supplier and well known in the market, so it was a bit intimidating. I was going up against a well-respected and long-standing brand, and I didn't know what to expect.

Flowflex took it on board. They explained they had an agreement with a guy called Richard Wragg, and he had a patent for the pipe cowl, which they were making under licence. Because of this, they thought they could not possibly be infringing my patent. I explained I thought differently and that they should reconsider. They wouldn't budge, so I took it up with my patent attorney, Steven McIlroy, of Murgitroyd & Co.

Steven was actually very confident that infringement was taking place. But I would need a barrister who practised English law because Flowflex was an English-based company. Steven and his colleague Stewart Cameron agreed that they would find a suitable barrister and a call was set up for all four of us to discuss the options.

Our barrister was called Miss Jane Lambert. She was very positive that we had a good case, and she agreed to represent me. So, the call was all very positive. However, I was sort of confused – Miss Lambert had very dulcet tones – her voice just didn't sound right to me. When she left the call, I raised this with Steven and Stewart, and they had a bit of a giggle. It turned out Miss Lambert was a man transitioning to a woman – hence her deep tones! I was a bit bemused, but if they were recommending her, then that was good enough for me. It was game on. The case was set for 9th August 2010 in Manchester, under Hearing Officer G. Elbrow.

The case hearing would start early, so I duly met up with Steven and Stewart in Manchester the night before. In the morning, we met Miss Lambert inside the venue. It was like a sort of council building with lots of people sitting about. Miss Lambert clearly looked like a man dressed as a woman. She was very pleasant and guided us through to where the hearing would take place. I couldn't help but notice that she had a ladder on the back of her tights. And that made me smile.

Proceedings began, and Miss Lambert was very good and very impressive. She dealt with all the technicalities of the law. Then it was my turn. I had to take the stand and explain in layman's terms why I felt that there was an infringement. I did this robustly, and the hearing officer commented on how explicit I had been.

The case went on all day. And at the end of it, the hearing officer found that an infringement had taken place. We had won! I was awarded £30,000, plus some costs.

I was a bit miffed about the decision on costs as I had forked out what must have been about £10,000 on the case. And on top of that, I had outlays for the two attorneys and the barrister as well as my own time. But the main thing was that I was vindicated.

Flowflex were all very amicable given they had just agreed to give me a lot of money, and I offered to sell them my rights to the patent for £1 million. They thought that was too high, so they refused. Over the course of the next few years, they approached me again, but I never lowered my price.

It turned out to be a mistake on their part. Over the years, I've received royalties from them and other parties in excess of the £1 million I asked for. They could have cornered the market and made a killing.

Royalties will continue until late 2023. Defending my patent rights turned out to be the right decision.

The house at Bothwell Road needed a lot of work and you can see 5 workmen hard at it.

22. BOTHWELL ROAD - PART 2: 2010 - 2013

U nder our management, Gas Call continued to expand and grow. We won lots of installation contracts, particularly for Aberdeenshire Council, which was a very rural area and hard to resource. It took a few months to get all the processes ironed out, but once we hit our stride, we ended up working there for five or six years. We turned out to be one of the best − if not the best − contractors that the council ever had. This allowed us to renegotiate our prices, and we made good profits on this contract.

It was about this time that we started entering business competitions across the country. I had got a taste of success from coming second in the Inner City 100 all those years ago, and now it was time to see if we could emulate that.

We entered the Herald Scottish Family Business Awards for several years in a row, and, of course, we were successful − we came second. And that was quite an achievement. We met the criteria because Vicki and Linzi both worked in the business before they moved on, and so did my sister and my niece, Ashleigh, and Mary's niece, Evonne. My brother Jim still worked with us; he commuted back and forth to Aberdeen. And Scott, the man Linzi would eventually marry, also worked for us. So, we really did meet the criteria for a family business!

We also pursued lots of health and safety awards because, obviously, health and safety is a big issue for most businesses, but it is especially important for us because of the nature of the work we do. I have never forgotten the devastation caused by the gas explosion at the Royal Darroch Hotel all those years ago, and I have always held our companies to the highest standards of health and safety.

Then we started entering international business awards, and we won with distinction, beating the likes of British Gas. We also entered some environmental awards, including VIBES (the Scottish Environment Business Awards).

We did very well in them all. It was great. When these awards come, you can either just accept the award and receive it through the post, or you can go and attend the ceremony. Of course, we went to the ceremonies – we were always up for a good time! We always took the family and a lot of the employees because without them, it would never have happened.

The awards were dished out at black-tie events in places like the Grand Central Hotel or the Hilton, and they were always spectacular. Everything was all dazzling and sparkly, and everybody enjoyed it. And, of course, we got involved in all the charity auctions and all that sort of thing. One year, we won an international safety award with distinction, through the British Safety Council. That award ceremony was held in the Dorchester Hotel in London. We had a great time. It was fantastic. We've got some great memories of all the family enjoying themselves because of what the business had achieved. And that only came about because of the success that we were creating – financial success as well as business success.

My son-in-law Alan was still with Liberty Gas and he was working away from home a lot, down in Wales and so on. And, of course, he had a wife to deal with in Glasgow, so it wasn't working out. He had to leave Liberty Gas and ended up working back 'on the tools' with Scottish Gas. But that didn't work out, either. Because he had been 'off the tools' and was now back 'on the tools', he was all over the place. It just wasn't right, and we had Vicki to think of, too. I decided to offer Alan his job back.

And slowly but surely, he got himself into the position where he is now running the business as Operations Director and helping to contribute to its ongoing success.

2013 was shaping up to be a very busy year, but it was also the year that Mary would turn 50, and I wanted to do something really special for her. I planned a surprise party with the girls, and for it, I got my pal Andy Kelly to compile a video of pictures that made up Mary's life story. It was to be accompanied by a new song I asked my old mentor, Ken Maclean, to write for her. It was a lot of work to try to get this all done without Mary finding out, but somehow I managed it. When the video was ready, I ran it past all the girls and they were blown away. They were all in tears, so it was clearly quite good. I could hardly wait to share it with Mary.

But first, I took her on a nostalgic cruise on the *Oceana*, because it was the first ship we had sailed on. We had a great time in the Mediterranean celebrating her birthday together, and everything was set for her surprise party on the day we got back from the cruise. Although I knew Mary wasn't really into parties, it was her 50th, so we had to do something special to mark the occasion. I knew she would enjoy it once it got started.

I had organised a limo to pick us all up at the house and drive us into town. Mary thought we had just planned a small private dinner in the Urban Brasserie in the city centre. Little did she know I had organised for all of her brothers and sister to be there! In the limo, it was party, party, party, with the champagne and beer flowing and all the loud music playing. It was a great start!

Her jaw hit the floor when she walked in and saw everyone waiting! She was not expecting that one! There were tears, of course, but they were happy tears. Making her happy was just such a good feeling. The setting was just perfect. The room was set out beautifully. There were balloons and a big cake decorated like a garden, and it even had a wee border collie on it like our dog, Bonzo. Everything was perfect.

Once everybody had composed themselves, I did a speech and a toast. Not so many nerves this time! At the end of the speech, I asked everyone to look up at the big screen that had been set up on one wall. First up was a great wee video that the girls had all put together, which made everybody smile. Then it was time for the new song and the picture show. The video was full of pictures and people that had been special to Mary throughout her life, like her mum, dad and gran. It went down a storm, and there wasn't a dry eye in the house.

My plan had worked! Then we had a great meal and partied the night away.

The whole thing had been a success, and we talk about it to this day.

One of the many Black & White tie family celebration nights. Seen here receiving an award in London.

23. BOTHWELL ROAD - PART 3: 2013- 2015

Work for Gas Call was increasing all the time, particularly in Aberdeen. We'd started the service and maintenance contract that we had won the year before, but I had an eye on the heating installations contract which we had been denied in 2008. We did eventually win it back, so it was a cause for celebration. Everything was going well in 2013.

However, it was not to last. The end of the year brought Mary some devastating news about her brother Jim.

He was a bricklayer, and he went to the doctor with pains. They did some tests, and he was told that, in fact, he had cancer. This was a massive shock to the whole family, particularly to his daughter, Claire. She was due to be married in the summer of 2014, and Jim was supposed to be walking her down the aisle.

Jim's disease progressed quickly, and he was admitted to the hospital and ended up in St Andrews Hospice in Coatbridge. They were very good, and they looked after him well. But it was very, very sad to watch Jim deteriorate so quickly. He was desperate to walk Claire down the aisle, but sadly, it wasn't to be. He passed away in April 2014, which was devastating for the whole family. Only months earlier, he had appeared fit and healthy, and now he was gone. I will always remember him and his cheeky grin and the fact he loved Coldplay before anybody else. Mary and I now love Coldplay, and we always think of Jim when we hear their music.

Mary's eldest brother, Matthew, was particularly hard hit by Jim's passing. He and his wife used to find solace in going to our caravan at Wemyss Bay, though sometimes, Matt would go on his own. He always expressed his gratitude for having a bolt-hole for whenever he needed space. It was the least we could do to help. It was just a sad, sad time.

Claire's wedding went ahead later that year. There is a very poignant picture of Mary and her sister, Esther, together with Matt and Gerard, her other brother. Jim was missing, but he should have been there. It should have been one of the proudest days of his life, walking his daughter, Claire, down the aisle. Life can be so cruel.

We finished the year with a weekend in London to celebrate our wedding anniversary. It was supposed to be the end of what was a very sad year for the family.

But 2014 hadn't quite finished with me yet.

Linzi was due to marry her fiancé, Scott, in February 2015, and I was to give a speech. After Vicki's wedding, I had vowed never to write my own speech again, so I engaged with a speech writer called Charlie McCarthy from a company called Blarney Patter. We arranged to meet up in the Millennium Hotel in George Square on 22nd December 2014, about two months before the wedding, to get everything sorted out and to give me time in practise. I parked the car in Mitchell Lane and headed up to George Square.

As I was walking through Royal Exchange Square, I could see a commotion ahead and a woman lying face down on the ground. Suddenly, Charlie appeared. He told me a bin lorry had run over several people, and there were fatalities. I was stunned. Charlie hurriedly explained he had to cancel our meeting because he was a nurse and he had to help deal with the carnage.

This turned out to be the day of the Glasgow bin lorry tragedy. And I had walked right into the middle of it. Shocked, I stood on the steps of the Royal Exchange Museum while people rushed back and forth. There were sirens blaring and blue lights flashing all around me. Six people were run down and killed by a bin lorry when the driver passed out at the wheel. They had simply been doing some last-minute Christmas shopping, and now their families would have to deal with this tragedy forever.

I phoned Mary to let her know what had happened, and I returned to the office in a state of shock. It was a day I would never forget.

Christmas came and went, and we were not sorry to see the end of 2014. I met up with Charlie in the new year, and he didn't talk much about that day. He must have seen some terrible sights.

But 2015 started with happier news. Not only did we have Linzi's wedding to look forward to, but in January, Kara told us she was pregnant!

For Scott and Linzi's wedding, we hired the Roman Camp Hotel in Callander for the whole weekend. On the day of the wedding, Linzi looked beautiful. But as we were walking down to the celebration room, she kicked off her very expensive wedding shoes! She actually got married in her bare feet, and nobody else knew!

My speech went down a storm at the wedding, which turned out to be a fantastic day. Some of my brothers questioned whether I had done the speech myself, but I never let on that Charlie had helped me!

Mary had secretly organised the secret waiters – a troupe of people who would act as waiters then suddenly break into song. They wowed the crowd. Even I was gobsmacked because I didn't know anything about it.

It was a great wedding.

And very soon after the wedding, Linzi was pregnant, too. And then Vicki was pregnant.

It was surreal. Three daughters all pregnant at the same time – it was crazy!

Mary and I had spent so many years when the girls were teenagers making sure they did not get pregnant, and they took this on board and got on with their careers instead. Vicki became a teacher, and Linzi became a nurse. Kara went to university and became a social worker. Mikaela, after several other jobs, eventually came to work for us at Gas Call, and she is there still.

They made us very proud, but as the years passed, we began to wonder if we would ever have grandchildren. And then, just like buses, three came along at once! To say it was a little challenging would be an understatement, but Mary and I were as proud as Punch, and we couldn't wait to meet all the new grandchildren.

Evie Ann McKenzie, the first, was born in September 2015. Harrison Donald Clarke was born in December 2015. And then Finlay Michael Lowe in January 2016.

A few years later, along came Fraser Joseph Lowe, a wee brother for Finlay, and then it was Isabella Mary Clarke, a wee sister for Harrison. And finally, wee Isla Mary McKenzie, a sister for Evie.

Mary took to her new role as a grandmother like a duck to water, and she has loved it ever since. It fills my heart to watch her interact with the children, and I love her all the more for it. As the band of grandchildren grew, we converted the old stables into a fabulous space for the family. It went over budget, but it was worth it in the long run, and we've had many happy times there. It's always been a great little den for the grandchildren and is full of wonderful memories and a fantastic picture wall of them all as they continue to grow.

L/R Kara, Linzi & Vicki all pregnant at the same time in 2015. Like buses none for ages then 3 at the same time.

L/R Fraser, Evie, Harrison, Isabella, Finlay & Isla. All growing up fast and great pals. The twins are yet to arrive.

Linzi and Scott on their wedding day at the Roman Camp in Callander.

24. BOTHWELL ROAD - PART 4: 2015- 2018

While life can be full of joy, it can also be full of sorrow. While we were welcoming the new members of our family with such happiness, more bad news was on the horizon.

Matt became unwell. After several tests, it was confirmed as cancer in his bladder. It was almost unbelievable that this was happening again, so soon after Jim.

Matt was a right old character. He was head of the family. The first time I met him at his house, I was warned that under no circumstances was anybody allowed to sit in Matt's seat. It was a big comfy armchair just beside the fireplace. After the introductions, I thought, *What the hell*, and I sat in the seat. There was a long silence. Then suddenly, he burst into laughter. The ice was well and truly broken! Me and Matt became good pals after that. If we were at a family function, we would always sit together and chat away. He was very well read and very knowledgeable and opinionated. Just my sort of guy. We got on great.

Matt was determined to fight the cancer and was stoic in his efforts. I recall we all attended a wedding at Cameron House on Loch Lomond. We stayed for a couple of days, and part of the time, we were out walking in the grounds. There was a wee seaplane on the loch, and I said to Matt, 'We should go up in that plane. It goes over the loch, and you get a bird's eye view.'

We decided we didn't have time because the weekend was extremely busy. So, we left it.

During his fight against cancer, I remember urging him that we should do the trip on the seaplane. We agreed that would be a good thing to do, but we never got around to it. Life was just too busy.

I went to visit him at home, and we had a good chat, despite his condition. I remembered how hugging my brother Arthur gave me some solace after my dad died, so when I was leaving, I said to him that I was gonna give him a man hug. He was quite taken aback. He was the head of the family; he was the big brother, and he'd always been quite tough. But he seemed comforted by the hug, and it's something I will always remember.

As Matt deteriorated, he would say his 'T was oot', which was quite a strange thing to say. It was like a realisation that he would soon be gone. It was a very sad time, particularly for Anne, Matt's wife, and his daughter, Evonne. To compound matters, Evonne was in the early stages of pregnancy. They were torn whether to tell Matt about the pregnancy. They didn't know if it would give him comfort or cause further anxiety because he wouldn't be around to meet his first grandchild. It was just tragic.

I remember my last visit to Matt in the hospice. He'd lost his hair, and he was making fun of it and all that sort of thing, trying to put on a brave face. We talked and laughed and shared a few tears. As we talked, he brought up the trip on the sea plane, and he said, 'We should have done that. It'd have been good fun.'

But now it was too late. There were tears in his eyes as he spoke, and that was one of the saddest moments in my life. Matt passed away a few days later. He was only 66. I had been privileged to know him, and I miss him to this day.

Mary was just devastated. It was only four years after Jim had died. It had been tragic to watch Matt go through the peaks of hope and troughs of despair during his chemotherapy. It was heartbreaking and painful being so helpless.

2018 was turning out to be quite a year. Matt's death had a big impact on both Mary and me. For years, we had spent most of our time in the business. Now we realised that life was short, and it was time to live our lives to the full. We had made our money. I had achieved my ambition, and I was a millionaire. Did we really want to spend what time we had left working our fingers to the bone? It was a big decision to make, but in the end, we decided to offload the business, take the money and enjoy life.

25. BOTHWELL ROAD - PART 5: 2018 - PRESENT

Once the news was out, we had several offers from PLCs and other private entities. But I had also reached out to Shaun Maclean. It turned out that Shaun was very interested. He and Martin Holmes, his business partner had sold Liberty Gas a few years earlier, and they were reaching the end of the covenants they had with Liberty, which meant the end of the non-competition clause. The covenants had prevented them being competitive within England — it didn't cover working in Scotland, so this was a good entry point back into the industry via the back door.

We engaged with Shaun and Martin via a new company they had created called the Duality Group. The guys were very impressed with our systems and people. It was incredible that we had turned the business around in a relatively short space of time. And now we were being rewarded.

Following on from a relatively short but intense due diligence process, we sold Gas Call Services back to the people who had sold it to us for £1 in 2010. And this time, we sold it in a multi-million-pound deal that would set us up for life.

This was effectively the third time we had sold Gas Call Services, and it was a success story by any measure.

I stayed on as consultant, director and shareholder of Duality. I knew the value of the group would grow, and, therefore, so would my stake in the business. The transition was easier than I expected. Shaun knew how I had run the business, so I was basically just left to get on with it. To appease the workforce and the clients, we dressed the deal up as a merger and not a sale. The workforce would have been unsettled if they knew the business had been sold again, and that would have had a negative impact.

Mary retired, and I sort of semi-retired. I was only going in for three days a week, Tuesday to Thursday, but as far as the clients were concerned, I was always available. Our business is a lot about relationships and stability, and my continuing relationship with the clients was an important part of the deal. It took a wee bit of getting used to, having worked hard all my life, but it allowed us to go away for long weekends and spend more time with our grandchildren.

The business continued to grow. In July 2019, we were awarded the contract for East Kent Housing in the southeast of England – the polar opposite of where we were working in Scotland. It was miles away. But we were used to working in rural locations, and that experience served us well in Kent.

We also agreed to take on all the Aberdeen City Council gas-related call handling, which meant we had to upgrade our call centre. We bought and installed a whole new telephone system that would help us produce reports and all that good stuff.

We had a record year in terms of turnover and profitability. Everything was going great, and the business continued to expand.

And then, of course, in March 2020, COVID hit.

The government set up rules to protect the population and limit the spread of the disease. The new rules meant that people should work from home where possible, so the call centre became redundant overnight. We had to start from scratch to meet the new regulations and keep the business going. That meant we had to install all sorts of new laptops and remote call software and train people to work from home. But despite all the challenges, it became an outstanding success. And to this date, we're still carrying on with the remote call centre process. This is despite the fact that, at the time of writing, all the COVID restrictions have been lifted. But the fact is, if it's not broke, don't fix it. It may be that we have to look at it going forward because, obviously, attitudes to work and working from home are changing, but this has certainly been an unmitigated success.

COVID also had an immediate impact on the gas business, but we were quick to react. We were deemed an essential service and had to continue our operations even though many other companies had to pause trading. Alan was excellent. He ensured we obtained suitable Personal Protective Equipment (PPE) for the workforce in the quantities we would require, and we bought more than we actually needed. But, with hindsight, that was a great idea.

As the pandemic grew, people were scared. We had to engage with the general public, and that was a high-risk operation because COVID was totally unknown then and there was major panic throughout the world. We introduced PPE, and we introduced new processes to safeguard our people and the public whose homes we had to enter. Despite all this, there was a lot of unrest and worry in the workforce.

To combat this, I quickly introduced a 10% increase in wages as a COVID-related bonus. This seemed to go down really well and had a very positive impact.

Unfortunately, we lost the 100% landlords' gas safety record with Aberdeen City Council. This was due to tenants being very reluctant to let our guys into the property, despite our processes. We would phone ahead of the visit; our guys would turn up in hazmat suits and all the rest of it – we took every precaution, but people were nervous or just weren't sure what was going on. Or perhaps they were vulnerable. But we got that rectified once the restrictions started to lift. By March 2022, we were back on track.

We are extremely proud of our workforce because, as a vital service, they had to rise above the call of duty to provide the services that were required. It was a scary thing, but they went above and beyond.

This is something for which I will always be truly thankful, so I would like to say well done to the team.

But COVID had even further consequences for me. In October 2020 my best pal and work colleague, Terry Maclean, who had recently retired, suddenly passed away. Due to ongoing COVID restrictions I couldn't attend his funeral in Dingwall. Instead, I had to attend remotely via a video link. I was devastated.

Then in May 2021 my other pal, Big Owen Burke, who had been with me for years since building Rhindmuir Grove, also passed away. Owen was a great guy and that was evident at his funeral, which was mobbed. About twenty of his workmates lined their Gas Call vans up in a makeshift guard of honour which brought tears to my eyes.

I miss my pals Terry and Big Owen very much.

26. CROFTMORAIG - 2019

I n the late summer of 2019, Mary decided to take a trip to Edinburgh. She was reading a magazine on the train, and she came across a property for sale. It was called Croftmoraig, and it was between Aberfeldy and Kenmore, an area where we'd spent many happy weekends with the family over the years. It was a great, great place and very special to us.

The first time I went to Glen Lyon was back in 1996. Mary, not for the first time, had rented a cottage with the two girls, and while they had set off in reasonably good weather, they encountered severe snow and blizzards on the way there.

When they arrived, Mary tried to light the fire with a match and some firelighters, but she was trying to light a damp log without any sort of kindling. She just didn't know what she was doing, and she was stuck. So, she called me to see if I would come and help to get this fire lit. Of course, given that I was on my own by this time and I'd never been there, I thought it might be a good wee adventure. So I headed up, and sure enough, there was loads of snow. It was like a single-track road, and it was treacherous. I thought how brave she must be to be making this journey. This was something that even I would fear, and she was up here on her own with Vicki and Linzi.

When I eventually arrived, I set about getting the fire lit because it was absolutely freezing. I showed Mary how to use kindling and start a fire, and to this day, she's as good a firelighter as I am. That was the first of many great times we've spent in Glen Lyon.

There was a wee post office with a shop attached, and we used to go there and have tea and cakes. They had wee seats outside, and it was lovely. Beside the post office, there was a swing on a tree, and we spent loads and loads of hours playing on it, having a good old laugh with the girls. It was great. There were rivers running by the cottage, and it was just really tranquil – a great place for getting away from it all, something we did regularly.

Over the years we had thought of buying something in the area, but there was never the opportunity, or the prices were ridiculous. We even considered buying the post office, at one point, but I was a city boy and I couldn't see myself as postmaster! But Mary had spotted Croftmoraig in the magazine, and she wanted to go and view it.

I made the arrangements right away. The property had recently been used as a holiday let, and it was very run down, but we saw the potential and Mary loved it and she wanted it. So that was that.

We eventually gave them an offer of £1,000 more than the asking price, and it was accepted. We were ecstatic. It turned out that Croftmoraig meant 'Mary's Croft', and the house had been built in 1957, which was the year I was born. It was almost like fate had taken a hand.

I spent the next few months or so travelling up and down, transforming the property into a beautiful house. Mary picked the fabrics and soft furnishings and the colour schemes, and we installed hot tubs and log fires and fire pits and put up swings for the kids. It turned out to be fantastic.

It's a great bolt-hole to get away to, and all the family have been up there. There are loads of memories, loads of photographs, loads of everything. It's absolutely idyllic, and I'm sure we'll enjoy many more good times to come. When we are at Croftmoraig, life couldn't be better.

Croftmoraig after we done lots of work to it including changing its colour. It is a fantastic getaway and very peaceful.

27. OLD LAWERS VILLAGE - 2021

Around midsummer in 2021, I read a newspaper article about an old, deserted village near Loch Tay that was for sale. It was called Old Lawers Village. I was fascinated. I went online and visited the website of the selling agent. On the website was a great video of the village, which was apparently haunted by the Lady of Lawers. She was a 17th-century prophetess and soothsayer who was said to haunt the village until her unfulfilled prophecy comes true. The soundtrack in the video was weirdly haunting, and it was really the music that caught my attention.

I thought about it for a day before mentioning it to Mary. I showed her the video and suggested I might want to buy it. She could see how interested I was, but she thought it was a bit mad to think of buying this old village. Especially since the sale of Old Lawers Village had gone viral, and there was a lot of interest from around the world. For me, it was an area we loved, and I was struck by the history of it. The fact that it was haunted made me very curious as well.

I've always been interested in ghosts, from when I was a small child. Over the years, there have been a few experiences that made me believe ghosts might actually exist, particularly when I was with Mary. Some of those were to do with her mum, who had passed away some years before.

I remember whenever we went to the Ho Wong restaurant and spoke about her mum, we would get a tingly sensation in the back of our necks that we believed meant Mary's mum was with us for some reason. Not in a bad way, of course. It was quite spooky, but it was nice to think of her being there with us. And there was a particular photograph we took at the graveyard. There was a stone wall behind the grave, and later, when we were looking at the picture, there were so many faces and people in the wall looking back, it was unreal. I showed that picture to my brother Arthur, and he could see all the faces as well.

Of course, that wasn't the only photographic proof. There was the picture I took when my mum died with the glow that I thought was her soul leaving her body at the moment of her passing. And there was another thing that happened when my mum died that involved Mary. It was when Mum was laid out in her coffin in the bedroom. All the family were in the front room together, except Mary. She was in the kitchen making a cup of tea. She came through with her tea, and without thinking, she sat in my mum's chair. Within seconds, she jumped straight out of the chair screaming and crying. She'd sensed that my mum had sat in the chair with her.

Mary was inconsolable. She was really spooked, and she swears to this day that my mother sat in the chair when she was in it.

Finally, Mary Donnelly, my brother's wife, has stuck by the story that she saw my dad floating up by the ceiling when he was lying in his coffin. That was just a bit crazy, but she maintains it was true.

All this has meant that I'm fascinated by ghosts, and for me, the village had that same kind of fascination. It was a chance to have my very own ghost. What else could I do? I bought it.

I had to pay a bit over the odds to get it because there was such high interest in it, but I wanted it. I wanted us to have it. I bought it without even viewing it, but when Mary and I went there for the first time, it was pouring with rain and there was a definite sense of spookiness about all the old buildings and ruins. It did feel haunted. I was well chuffed.

While this was all going on, COVID had wreaked havoc on the world and our business. But one of the biggest disappointments was that Kara's pending wedding to John McKenzie had been postponed, not once but twice. Kara had met John through her social network, and for her wedding, she had planned a big splash at the Meldrum House Hotel in Aberdeenshire. But because there was such turmoil in the whole world at that point, and particularly in Scotland, where the laws were different from the rest of the country, nobody knew what was going on. The dates came and went, and it left them very anxious.

Eventually, some of the restrictions lifted, and the big day was upon us. We arranged to have a family meal at the hotel the night before. Ann had remarried, so she would be there with her new husband, Taffy. It was a bit strange being in the same room with Mary and Ann and Taffy, but it all passed off very amicably.

The wedding was held on 1st August 2021, and it was a great success. Kara was a beautiful bride, and Vicki and Linzi and Mikaela all looked fabulous as bridesmaids. Evie and Isla were flower girls, and they were as cute as anything. All the men and boys were wearing kilts and trews, even the grandchildren.

It was a bit strange having to wear a mask as we walked down the aisle, and there were also other restrictions in place during the service. It was very strange because of the whole COVID thing, and it was emotional as well. COVID had touched all of our lives so deeply over the past two years, keeping us apart at times, and now here we all were, together at last to celebrate Kara and John's wedding. Mikaela had written some poems that were read out, and it was all very nice. I was tasked with looking after Isabella. We were in the front row, and she was a little angel – not! But we all had a great time. My speech (again with the assistance of Charlie!) seemed to go down well. And there was no heckling, as such, so it must have been not too bad!

We partied into the wee small hours, and by then, all the masks had disappeared and it turned out to be a normal wedding with all the traditional songs.

Mikaela is the only one not married yet, and as far as I know, she has no current plans to get married anytime soon. She is loving life with Bowie, her black lab, who's a very energetic big rascal. Cupid's arrow still has to land in Mikaela's heart, but I'm sure she will meet the man of her dreams soon enough. She has actually started dating recently so we will see how that goes. We'll keep Charlie's number on speed dial just in case!

L/R: Linzi, Vicki, Mary, Mikaela & Kara. All my girls enjoying some fun time in Edinburgh before Kara's big day.

Me with Kara and John on their Wedding Day. It was 3rd time lucky after being postponed twice due to COVID.

28. REFLECTIONS ON MY LIFE

The city I was born into was full of smoke and dirt and poverty. But Glasgow has come a long way since 1957. It has made its way in the world and is now a bustling city full of life and vigour, a European City of Culture and a city of the Commonwealth Games. A city of business and drama and music and light.

And I have come a long way on my journey from that tenement flat in Springburn, all the way to Bothwell Road and Old Lawers Village. I left school with no qualifications and no academic skills. I was just a boy from Springburn, like so many others, out to make his way in the world. The difference is that I knew what I wanted very early in life. My ambition was to be a millionaire before I was 50. And that I did.

One of my favourite sayings is 'work hard and you get rewarded', and that's certainly been the case for me. It was all about attitude, hard work, timing and luck. My plan was always to build the business to a level where I could sell it, and that would make me financially secure. I was never going to be a poor pensioner! The fact that I've done it three times is a testament to my success. But it wasn't easy. I remember being 'on the tools' and the call outs on Christmas Day, and how it felt to begin again. And then success came, and I sat at Jack McConnell's desk in Holyrood when he was first minister. There were stories about me in *The Herald* newspaper, and Heriot-Watt University even did a paper on me. And then there were all the black-tie nights out to recognise and celebrate our achievements.

Over the years, I've created hundreds of jobs, and through those jobs supported many, many families and contributed to the wealth of the country through tax. But with success comes responsibility, and we try and give back where we can. Losing two brothers as we did through cancer led us to get involved with the St Andrew's Hospice. We've made quite a lot of donations to them over the years. And we are investigating how to donate defibrillators in our area to support the national network.

But for all that, it's the times spent with family that stand out. My dad always said, 'Look after your own,' and I have been glad to share my financial success with my family. Part of that is my table at Celtic Park that all the family use. It feels good to do something my dad instilled in me. There have been a few run-ins with the family over the years for one reason or another, but we've always got together in the end. We've generally managed to stay on good terms, and I'm glad to say that they are mostly in good health, except for my brother Jim, who was unfortunately diagnosed with lung cancer. That came as a shock after losing Mary's brothers to cancer, but the outcome for Jim is positive. The operation to remove 50% of his lung and some lymph nodes was a success, and the cancer has gone. He has started chemotherapy as a precautionary measure, and we expect he will be with us for many years to come.

Gas Call has continued to go from strength to strength, and I'm enjoying my new role. Since I am only working three days a week, I have plenty of time to put into Old Lawers Village. I've set up our website at www.oldlawersvillage.co.uk, and I've commissioned a reimagined scale model of the village showing what it might have looked like back in the day. The model will be available to view at the new Crannog Centre, which is currently being built on Loch Tay. But that's just the beginning. I've lots of plans for the old village. I want to protect it for future generations because it's part of Scotland's heritage, so I'm working with the appropriate bodies and we'll see how that goes.

I'm also looking forward to spending more time on the beach with our wonderful grandchildren to give them and us some great memories. They are growing up so fast, and the family is continuing to grow – on 15th November 2022 Linzi gave birth to twin girls, Rosie Maria and Sofia Victoria. The thought of eight grandchildren is mind-blowing. Mary is in her element, and she says the grandchildren keep her young. You can tell that's the case just by looking at her. In my opinion, she would win any 'glamourous granny' competition hands down!

Everybody's well placed for the challenges of life. You always want to see your kids do better than you've done in life. And hopefully, I've achieved the kind of success that will ensure that. But I couldn't have done it without the support from my family, which I've had in spadefuls at every turn. Especially from Mary. I couldn't have made this journey without her. From the moment I met her, her input and support have been unending, not to mention the grand job that she did in helping us build the business. She has truly been my partner in every way.

I have always wanted to write a book about my life but never had time to do so until now. It's like I have it all except time. My life has always been busy, and I've never had to wonder where the years went. My mum used to tell me my job would always be there even when I wasn't, and that time gets faster and passes quicker as you get older. These were words of wisdom, and she was not wrong. I spent most of my life working hard and creating success, and now I've spent the last part of my life trying to make good memories for the family so they can look back and hopefully see that life has been fun, too.

There's a song by Dido called 'Life for Rent', and there's a lyric in it that says, 'Nothing I have is truly mine.' This is the way I've always thought. You're born with nothing, and you die with nothing – no pockets on a shroud, as they say. So, the only things you own are your memories, and it is up to you to make sure they are good.

For anyone reading this, I think the message is no matter where you start in life, if you apply yourself and work hard, anything is possible, and with success comes reward. I wanted my story to be inspirational, and I hope that it is.

And for me, the journey continues.

L/R: Francis, Brian, My nephew Ross, (Marie was working) Christine, Jim &
Arthur enjoying the hospitality at Celtic Park

L/R: Scott, Linzi , Mary and Me at Celtic Park enjoying the football.

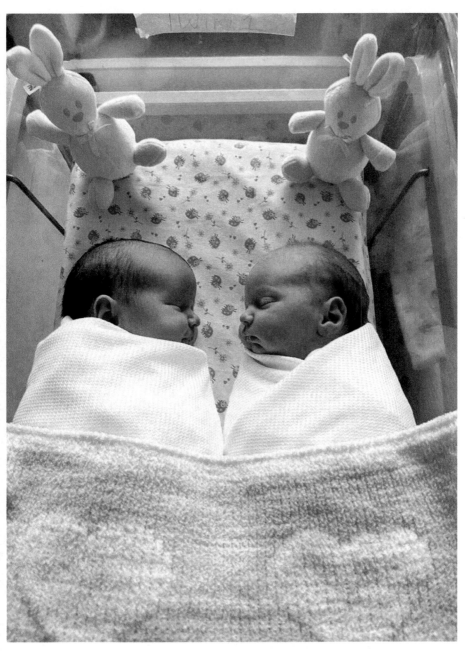

L/R: Sofia and Rosie still in the hospital looking forward to going home.

Me and Mary. Very proud Grandparents with the Twins Sofia and Rosie.

ACKNOWLEDGEMENT

Within these pages, I have tried to provide a backdrop to my life so far. From the very early days, I was inspired by my circumstances and in particular my upbringing by my Mum and Dad and the values they instilled in me, along with their hard work and fortitude. Their guidance, and the memories they created for me and my brothers and sisters in such hard times, were nothing short of exceptional.

When I look back over the years there have been many key events that ultimately helped to shape the person I have become. Most notably the deaths of my parents, which had a big impact on me. My Dad died suddenly but my Mum's death was expected. These were two very different experiences but to this day I follow their guidance and still quote, and do, a lot of what they imparted to me. This has helped me to carve out a successful career over the years, well beyond what they probably thought was possible. I still miss my parents, Frank and Betty, and wish they had seen my success. To them, I will be forever grateful.

My story should inspire anyone reading it. It demonstrates that no matter what your background is you can succeed in life. A lot of success is down to timing and luck but without hard work, determination and the support of those around you it would be almost impossible.

SPRINGBURN TO LAWERS

Story Terrace

Printed in Great Britain
by Amazon